Praise for *Be More Wrong*

"*Be More Wrong* is a refreshing change from the books that promise better leadership in three easy steps. This is an invaluable manual for those leaders who are ready to experiment and get it wrong in service of getting it right."

Liane Davey, author, *You First* and *The Good Fight*

"In the post-COVID world where disruption across societies, industries, and the world of work will be the norm, the successful leader will disrupt, have purpose, be data driven, and champion talent. Colin Hunter offers a powerful approach to building this new leadership DNA. Drawing from his deep experience, Colin offers real insight, great stories, and, importantly, practical advice. A top read for someone wanting to start their leadership journey in a fresh new way or for a seasoned leader ready for reinvention."

Ismail Amla, coauthor, *From Incremental to Exponential*

"*Be More Wrong* shows how the path to unparalleled success is paved with purposeful failure. In this sweeping, original, and slyly subversive book, Colin Hunter shares fresh insights and practical guidance that you can use to inform, enrich, and enliven your leadership adventures. It's a rare treat to find yourself being provoked, agitated, and challenged... and being eager for more as you turn each page. You couldn't do more right than to read *Be More Wrong*!"

Bill Treasurer, author, *Courage Goes to Work*

"*Be More Wrong* provides a road map to a leadership style that ensures innovation, satisfaction, growth, and happiness. It delivers a framework to help leaders see how they can 'be more wrong' to learn quickly and achieve success. This is not just another leadership book. It is one you'll want to read carefully, mark up the margins, and try out the suggested habits."

Elaine Biech, author, *Skills for Career Success*

**be
more
wrong**

How Failure Makes You an Outstanding Leader

be more wrong

COLIN HUNTER

Foreword by Michael Bungay Stanier

● ● PAGE TWO

Cataloguing in publication information
is available from Library and Archives Canada.
ISBN 978-1-77458-039-4 (hardcover)
ISBN 978-1-77458-040-0 (ebook)

Page Two
pagetwo.com

Edited by James Harbeck
Copyedited by Steph VanderMeulen
Proofread by Alison Strobel
Jacket design by Taysia Louie
Interior design by Fiona Lee
Interior illustrations by Michelle Clement
Printed and bound in Canada by Friesens
Distributed in Canada by Raincoast Books
Distributed in the US and internationally by Macmillan

21 22 23 24 25   5 4 3 2 1

BeMoreWrong.com

MY FAVORITE EXPRESSION when coaching leaders is "Knowledge speaks, wisdom listens," by Jimi Hendrix. I could have dedicated this book to all the people you hear mentioned in its chapters who shaped my journey of being more wrong. However, there is one person, more than any other, who influenced me in my life and leadership journey—and that is Randy Taylor. He was a student of my grandfather's and took me into his home in the United States just after college. He and his wife, Arline, made me feel like a member of their family. I have held a vision of him in my mind, from that time: he's sitting on a rocking chair on a deck in Montreat, North Carolina, smoking his pipe, laughing and listening with an assured curiosity to my twenty-one-year-old, insecure self starting out on a journey that is now my working life. Randy had the amazing ability to make me feel special, to make my stories feel interesting, to make my questions on politics and life feel like the most inspired questions ever. He made everybody he met feel special in their own right, whether they agreed with his views or not. By truly listening, he recruited them as followers. By being curious, he mentored me on how to observe, listen, and create new insights from differing points of view. He sought out the tough conversations and allowed himself to be more wrong and see others' views. He was a leader I could admire, a person I could look up to, and to all his family and friends, a person who filled their lives with laughter, wisdom, and love.

Contents

"Only a small part is played in great deeds by any hero."

GANDALF, *The Lord of the Rings: The Fellowship of the Ring*

foreword

I'VE BEEN WRONG about almost everything.

About the job I'd end up having. What I'd be good at. What would bore me. Where I'd have success. Where I'd fail. How I'd lead. Where I'd end up living. What I'm known for. What would be important to me when I was thirty, and then forty, and then fifty.

And that's just a few things about me. Don't even get me started on how many ways I've been wrong about things about my wife...

But "wrong" isn't the most interesting word in the title of Colin Hunter's book. It's "more." Be more wrong.

In other words, it's not just "accept that you won't get everything right and hope that no one important enough notices." No, what we have here is a gauntlet laid down: get better at being wrong. Do it faster and more courageously and with greater gusto.

There's a reason for this seemingly nonsensical advice. It's that out there on the edge, at the boundaries of the map, in the water just out of your depth, across the threshold of the hero's journey... that's where your best self is to be found.

If you're considering *Be More Wrong*, it's because you're a leader seeking to be better.

You can only go so far as a leader through learning the technical skills. Those are the ones you get right, and my guess is you've mostly mastered those. That's where we all start, but make no mistake: they're just the start. The juicy, interesting stuff is off the expected path. It's in the place you learn to be more wrong about your own and others' expectations, and more right about the leader the world is asking you to be.

MICHAEL BUNGAY STANIER,
author of *The Coaching Habit* and *The Advice Trap*

prologue
from playground to work . . . to playground again

WHEN I WAS twenty-nine years old, I collapsed on a golf course. It was the start of a breakdown that ended with me driving all the way from Nottingham, where I lived, to Newcastle and falling apart in front of my parents. I could not cope and I did not know why.

I was working for Procter & Gamble in a medical representative sales role that I hated. I was burning the candle at both ends, also socializing, trying to find a group of friends in a new city. I was exercising, but my diet was mixed and my lifestyle did not include recovery. I ended up sitting in front of our family doctor, Gus Da Silva. It was his conversation and guidance that changed my life and started me on a new journey. I was unhappy in my job and did not know why. My resilience was low and I needed to change. Dr. Da Silva said that I needed to manage my energy and find a way to take better care of myself. How could I have fun in what I did and how could I build myself up to be more resilient to what life threw at me?

My collapse on the golf course triggered the recognition that something was wrong—that I was wrong. Out of being wrong, I sought to change my life: I decided to do an MBA, decided to be myself for that MBA year, and with all of that, made new connections without which I would not have found that first meaningful leadership consultant role. By being wrong, I had found my place to make a difference. That journey from Nottingham to Newcastle turned out to be the start of a longer, continuing journey of personal evolution that has guided my professional choices in the vast playground that most of us call work.

Playground? Yes. Work may seem a lot like school but, when I look back at my school days, I remember one part of them fondly: break times in the playground—morning break, lunchtime, and afternoon break. Why? Because that was when we had fun. The games we played, the laughs we had, the fights that started over nothing, and the banter. We came back to the classroom for a rest. We had taken a risk, had mud on our knees and a smile on our face.

The more I have worked in and with organizations, the more I have realized how deeply unhappy a lot of people are at work. Why should this be? All of the elements of playground fun exist at work—competition, games, banter, risk, teams—and yet . . .

My thinking from this time, and more specifically over the last few years, has been that the future of organizations lies in both finding a way to allow their people to be more resilient and also to create a playground environment where people can play, learn, push the boundaries, stretch themselves, love their work, and be happy.

My journey to creating a playground to disrupt the way people are led began at The Oxford Group, a consulting and training company, where I was a leadership consultant. This eventually led to me starting my own company, Potential Squared International, and to the book you now hold. I am not saying that every day I bounce into work happy and feel sad leaving. I am saying that I found a niche where I could create heroes of the people I work with, and also where I could experiment and fail with many ways to disrupt how people are led.

The vital ingredient, which was there at the beginning but not clear to me until much later in the journey, was that you have to fail to succeed. In fact, you have to fail quite a lot to really make a difference. In my career to that point, I had had many failures in how I had carried out my various roles and led teams, and also in how I had lived my life. But I had taken risks, been wrong, and benefited massively from it.

From Playground to Work—What's Right about Being More Wrong?

Imagine sitting in your favorite coffee house early one morning, reflecting on a tough day with your team the day before. You delivered some harsh truths, but it was done the right way. Then one of your leadership team pops into the cafe, sits down, and says to you in a friendly but direct way, "About yesterday. You couldn't be more wrong!"

That actually happened to me twenty-two years after I had found my playground. It was important for me to know, and important that it could be said to me by one of my team. But "You couldn't be more wrong!" is usually a dagger to the heart because, if it is true, the truth is hard to swallow. Which also implies there's something fundamentally not right with being wrong.

The feeling I had about five minutes later is the foundation of this book. I am a leader, and being more wrong has a powerful and proper role to play in my leadership. By "being wrong," I had been a catalyst for the team and myself to change. Being wrong is about discovery. This book describes the journey of that discovery and how I have concluded that being wrong is a good thing.

Sure, being wrong means you've tested something out and it's failed. Sometimes that has an impact on people that is not great—in some cases, it's painful. But knowing you're wrong always means that you and others have learned something in the process. More importantly, reframing failure as something useful means you're not afraid to take risks, and that's a powerful thing.

People want to learn and grow at their own pace and in their own way. They are willing to take a risk if that risk is mitigated and in a place of safety—like the playground at school. That playground was supervised: it allowed people to choose their game—or to choose to shoot the breeze about music or the latest film. It was a learning ground. Your level of ability mattered there (I was last to get picked for certain games) and your team members relied on you to perform and collaborate. But the outcome was never life-threatening. You could fail and still live to fight or play another day.

Together, my experiences of being wrong and of the playground have led me to crystallize my purpose for my business, which is to create a measurable playground to disrupt the way people are led. (The "measurable" is there for a reason, and I will come back to it.) My method is to guide leaders in creating their own playgrounds that allow their people to disrupt the way they do business—in other words, to guide leaders in the creation of cultures that thrive on putting the user at the center of their work, and on failing forward with those users to create fantastic new solutions and products.

Followers might be drawn to sign up for a journey because of the leader's purpose. Most important is that they understand the rules they must play by, and they have a clear understanding of what is expected of them—just as in a playground. One of the first models I ever used as a consultant—the Leadership Paradox—brings this to life very well. The paradox in this case is the balance of giving people a clear sense of direction but also the freedom to act, and possibly fail. And in embracing failure like this, it is but a short step to the concept of "fail faster to succeed sooner." That's now a core principle in Design Thinking, a field of innovation attributed to David Kelley, founder of IDEO, an international design and consulting firm. Its popularity is increasing with engineers and industrial and process designers.

However, this mantra, fail faster to succeed sooner, so crucial to start-up businesses, is possibly the most underemployed mindset in modern business. And for an obvious reason: most people are so scared of failing that they never test or experiment. Maybe their leader hasn't given them permission to fail—or tells them they can but then tells them off when they do.

Creating the future is always exciting. Disrupting the current state for the good of others and the world is what leadership is all about: it is one of the most common statements of purpose articulated by the leaders I meet. Doing what they do for others is at the heart of the hero's journey. The leader becomes the guide who creates the conditions for their followers' work to be successful.

So how does a leader do this? Conditions are shaped by a leader's own actions. You have to start with yourself—I learned that while sitting in front of my family doctor. You have to start by forming habits and systems to support your changes and to make yourself resilient in the face of failure. In other words, the habits and systems you create in your team and with your customers establish the conditions of change for good. In their works on habits, authors such as James Clear, Charles Duhigg, and B. J. Fogg tell us that creating changes in behaviors, habits, and systems requires us to have others in mind. The more reading and work we do in this area, the more we find it is the missing link for many leaders. We send leaders on courses, they learn and apply possibly two or three new things, and then they forget it all. Making those changes sustainable requires the creation of systems and habits, which requires a purpose focused on others.

Agitating for the Future

What is leadership? I define it as "agitating for the future." Leadership is about the art of future-proofing your organization. The essential question is: How can you peek around the corner and see what is coming?

I am reminded of a text from a colleague stating that the workshop he was running, entitled "Horizon Scanning," had been canceled ironically due to "unexpected circumstances." As the old saying goes, "It is difficult to make predictions, especially about the future"—and many times, leaders base predictions just on what has happened in their past. But as Nassim Nicholas Taleb says in his book *Antifragile*, it is impossible to accurately predict the future from what we have seen in the past. Thus, he says, we need to ensure that the systems we have and the people we work with are, at best, antifragile—more resilient to ride the waves of change in the future.

Design Thinking is one tool leaders can use to apply a growth mindset to the future and to craft breakthrough products, solutions, or ways of working. In sport, for example, Sir Dave Brailsford has driven success in cycling by searching for and implementing incremental changes that give his teams the edge, innovating not just the fueling system but also the types of pillows and even separate washing machines for each cyclist. Leaders such as Brailsford are constantly experimenting to shape the future edge in sport. His success with the INEOS Grenadiers cycling team has fluctuated, but he and the team use each failure to learn honestly and move forward.

In the past, it has been the organization's and leader's goal to come up with new ideas without making mistakes. How can we launch the perfect new product or service without being wrong? Now, we have learned that it is pretty much an impossibility. In fact, to come up with the small or large changes, we need to consciously fail ugly and early in what we do.

It is amazing what a growth mindset and creating a playground can do for your leadership. For example, I never thought fifteen years ago I would be meditating my way to success—or celebrating failure. But both have helped me immensely. Yet, how often as leaders do we feel we can play and try something new? We usually take the path of least resistance and do what we have always done. We have lost the exuberant freedom of playing on the playground because we are terrified of failure.

There's plenty of literature out there on the benefits of failing faster to succeed sooner. This book is about how to fail faster as a leader, and create a "fail fast" revolution for your team and your customers. My argument is that successful leadership is fundamentally about failing, learning, improving, testing, and being ready to either succeed or fail again. As Ozan Varol put it in his book *Think Like a Rocket Scientist*, it is about being more wrong so we can learn fast.

From Work to Playground Again: The Hero's Journey

For me, and for many of the leaders I coach and mentor, leadership is a never-ending adventure filled with joy, perils, thrills, and excitement. With this book, I want to refresh the role of leader with a sense of that excitement and thrill, setting it within the context of a wider cultural narrative while still acknowledging the thinking that is being done to enhance our approach to the different elements of that role.

Cultures around the world throughout history have had a concept of the hero's journey. The principles of the hero's journey remain the same: the hero gets a call to adventure (because of a threat), is driven by purpose, gathers followers, meets a guide, crosses the threshold, faces challenges, has successes and failures, is helped by a wider group of followers, grows new skills, transforms, returns changed, tells the story, and the cycle goes on. In short, it is an adventure guided by the hero's purpose through which those on the journey are transformed.

You can recognize this hero in popular fiction: consider Frodo in *The Lord of the Rings* or Harry Potter. The hero leaves home (Hobbiton or Privet Drive) on a purposeful adventure, is joined by others (chiefly Sam, Merry, and Pippin; Hermione, Ron, and Neville), has a quest (to destroy the ring or defeat Voldemort), faces good and evil, fails and learns, has a guide who helps them (Gandalf; Dumbledore), and returns forever changed.

We all know of real-life heroes and their journeys. And all heroes go through a version of this journey: consider Greta Thunberg, Mahatma Gandhi, Nelson Mandela, Richard Branson, and Steve Jobs. Their journey is an important part of how we see and understand them. And many people benefit from and are inspired by their stories.

But what does this have to do with being more wrong? As Will Smith puts it, "Fail early, fail often, fail forward": live at the edge of your capability, stretch it, and learn as you progress. Smith is giving personal advice, but it also holds true for team leaders. The hero's journey, with its trials and errors, is a framework for leadership, and for being more wrong. It is not about sailing your ship in the harbor where the waters are calm—it's about testing yourself when in rougher seas, pushing the boat to the limits, finding new ways to test the crew, new ways to go faster or to create an edge in what you do, always with a clear purpose and laser focus to stretch specific behaviors or test the team. There are times when getting barnacles on your butt and replenishing your resources in a safe harbor might be necessary. But the buzz of the team and the feeling of being part of something alive is what appeals to you and your crew. Imagine if Frodo had stayed at home in Hobbiton, if Harry Potter had lived with his horrible aunt and uncle and never gone to Hogwarts—or if Edmund Hillary had stayed at home with his bees and not climbed Everest. We would never have heard of Tenzing Norgay, of Hermione Granger and Neville Longbottom, of Aragorn or Merry and Pippin.

It's not all great battles and epic moments, however. It can be small things, the move toward what Brailsford, in his work, calls "incremental gains." The focus on purposeful practice and honing small elements of the team's or product's effectiveness allows the team to raise their game. The smallest changes sometimes make the biggest difference. But they need to be made with a clear purpose in mind. Is it to win the America's Cup in sailing? To make the first truly electric car? To truly democratize the Design Thinking process to the world, or to create a measurable playground to disrupt the way people are led? Let me say it again: the way to do it is to sail your ship out of the harbor, risk being wrong, and purposefully stretch the systems and habits in your team to be successful.

The Unlikely Leader

By now you are asking yourself who qualifies for this daunting and exciting role of leader, guide, or hero. There is much written on the different kinds of leaders, but the scale of the achievements and reach of the leaders we look up to makes our small view seem insignificant and incomparable. But they, too, started somewhere in a "village." They, too, stepped over the threshold and had their failures and traumas along the way. Harry Potter was an unwanted, unpromising child; Frodo Baggins was an ordinary hobbit living a comfortable life; Edmund Hillary was a beekeeper in New Zealand.

In reality, unlikely leaders exist everywhere, and they're disrupting the way we do things every day. They may be demonstrating imposter syndrome—a psychological pattern in which an individual doubts their skills, talents, or accomplishments and has a persistent internalized fear of being exposed as a "fraud." I suffer from this all the time in my role, especially when working at board level.

These heroes, these leaders, are not necessarily wearing a power suit. They're connecting with people and energizing them to go out and live, learn, and thrive the right way—which a lot of the time seems the hard way—because they know that failure, usually inevitable at least some of the time, produces the strongest insights. They may feel sure that they're the wrong person for the leadership job, but they're doing it anyway.

If you feel any empathy for the unlikely leader, then this book is for you.

"Agitating for the future" means disrupting yourself, your team, and your clients before somebody else disrupts you. It is at their most successful times that leaders need to stand up and disrupt the team around them. The amount of fear they have to overcome in order to do so is up to them and how well they have tested and stretched themselves in their lives. This is a book for leaders who don't just want to create change (all leaders do): they also want to—or have to—embark on an adventure, sail their ship out of the harbor, ride the waves, and take themselves and their team further than they ever thought they could.

As a leadership consultant, my job is to guide clients and their people, as well as my own team, to a place they never thought they could get to. The really satisfying part is when they wonder why they ever lived where they did before. This goal is part of a leader's role as well, and in leaders' tales of success, it is my experience that you will find many examples of being more wrong.

So how do you do this "be more wrong" thing?

If the Leadership Paradox I mentioned earlier was my first light bulb moment for my thinking on leadership, then Design Thinking was a close second in the evolution of the Pi2 Leadership Impact Model at the core of this book. Design Thinking is an iterative process or a series of habits that you can deploy to create "human-centered innovation." Its value as a process lies in its ability to be seen as a set of habits that can be used separately or combined. The fact that the habits are in a logical order should be prefaced with one of my favorite mindsets—that is, being "all prepared for your spontaneity session." Being willing to stop, pause, reflect, and possibly even go back a step if necessary is critical to the system. You must leave your ego and expertise at the door as you and your team embark on a journey to observe human behavior, create insights on observations, form new ideas, invent prototypes, and experiment. To venture beyond where you currently are, you must create products and solutions that you had not thought possible or even imagined existed.

Once you have had the taste of Design Thinking and learning fast, you, your team, and your customers will never want to go back to how things were. With one of our key clients, Akamai, we failed our way over four years from minimal offerings to award-winning leadership experiences that got everyone involved salivating at the thought of more new changes and stretched boundaries. This is the spirit of being more wrong.

the playground at work

the leadership impact model (Pi2)

I WAS FASCINATED BY a conversation with a friend whose son was attending a soccer academy with one of the big clubs in the United Kingdom. We were talking about what it takes for young players to rise through the ranks and succeed and the stories of the successful players who started with less talent than their peers and came out as the better players. What made the difference in these success stories? Was it the person who led the academy? Was it something about the individual player?

The conversation turned to what it takes to be successful in the sport. Talent is surely a given, we decided. Attitude and hard work, and even the luck of being in the right place at the right time. Their teammates, too: If they are surrounded by great players, then surely they too thrive? But then, all of that often seems to count for nothing when they leave that club or when the club's manager changes. Good players suddenly become ordinary. Success is affected by so many things.

The same sorts of arguments have been raised and discussed on the topic of successful leaders. Are they born or can they be developed? Do they become great leaders because they are around other great leaders? Does their upbringing help or hinder them from becoming a great leader? When Jack Welch was leading GE to great success, the company created a succession plan, with three candidates being groomed for the CEO role. In theory, the brains and other factors were all there for it to be successful. But it was not. What went wrong?

It reminds me of a classic story—Jamie Smart mentions it in his book *Clarity*. A drunk man is scrabbling around under a streetlight. A policeman comes up to him and asks him what he is doing. "I'm trying to find my keys," the man says. "Where did you lose them?" asks the policeman. "Over there!" says the drunk man, pointing into the darkness. "So why on earth are you looking here?" asks the policeman. The drunk man looks up at him incredulously and gestures at the lamp: "Because the light is better here!"

There have been more than a few times in my career as a leader when I wanted some sort of framework or guide to tell me how to deal with things and make decisions. Just like the drunk man, I looked where the looking was easiest: I sought the tried and tested lists of leaders I respected, only to find that, just as happened to GE, they all sounded smart but did not work for me. I left the frameworks behind, assuming that my lack of success was my fault—things failed because I lacked talent. The one time I felt I had a framework that worked was when I was being led by Ian Ritchie, my former manager. He had a way of crafting different frameworks for me around different areas, from sales to people. But when he left, so did his systems.

And so I needed to stumble around in the darkness if I was going to find the key. I needed to find my framework through practice and experiment. I needed to be wrong, more wrong, and even more wrong still. I needed it for myself and for all those who, like me, felt like unlikely leaders.

The fact is that plans built on what worked in the past tend to struggle when they come into contact with the current reality. As the old military saying goes, "No plan survives first contact with the enemy." Systems and habits must be adaptable to allow individuals to be successful. We just need to experiment with what works, be more wrong, and find the right mixture for us to achieve our quest.

We also need to be well prepared to be spontaneous. Otherwise, as James Clear says, we won't rise to the level of our goals; we'll fall to the level of our systems.

When you look in leadership books and on websites, there is normally a list of, say, five things that great leaders do. It is fascinating to explore those five things and try to do them. You will typically find that these particular five things are insufficient for your purpose. Problems come in many ways. There are many issues you could encounter that nobody has written about. Most leaders inherit teams, situations, clients, or problems; in some cases they inherit successes. The five things someone else did to be successful are more than likely not, as written, the five things that will contribute to your success or take your team to the next level. There might be something behind them that might be useful. But you will need to put their points of view or habits into practice and see what works for you and what you learn fast from being more wrong.

The book that has best clarified my thinking on how to deploy successful leadership is *Atomic Habits* by James Clear. He brings the philosophy that to be successful is a lifelong journey based on robust tested systems and habits. Therefore, finding the habits and systems that set you up for long-term success is your goal as a leader, however unlikely you see yourself for the role.

This book sets out the systems and habits I found that would help me, and other unlikely leaders, be sustainably successful.

The Evolution

Before I came across the work of James Clear, my team and I had been evolving our own work around a leadership system and exploring varying works on habits. Our model has its origins in our work on executive presence. I had been introduced to the dimensions of prominence and gravitas in executive presence (which I will be telling you all about) by my colleague Jacqueline Farrington of Farrington Partners. Another colleague, Tom Heywood, and I decided to take this further and explore how gravitas and prominence

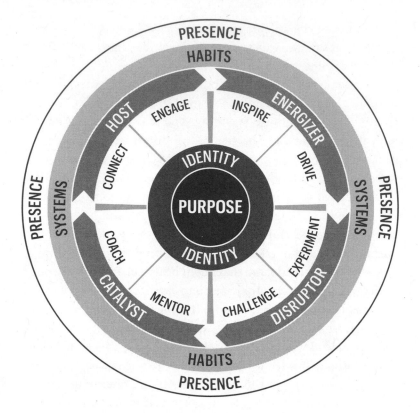

interact. That work was developed into a very successful program we still run today. One of the main reasons it is successful is that it gives leaders dimensions within a system to assess their own preferences, systems, and habits. It also allows them to have some parameters to flex their approach and therefore their impact on their team and customers.

The interaction of these two dimensions created quadrants that we labeled the four styles for leaders to measure themselves against. These styles are Host, Energizer, Disruptor, and Catalyst. The system became the Leadership Impact Model that we call Pi2 (for Potential Impact Squared). At its core, the Pi2 model has habits and systems that, if lived, provide a vibrant leadership impact. It also embodies three enablers that provide confidence, conviction, and connection in how you deliver your styles to the world: purpose, identity, and presence. And finally, there is a fourth element that facilitates the smooth play of the whole model: refreshingly direct conversations.

Once we had a framework—like a bridge—we needed to explain it through stories—a vehicle to cross the bridge. That's where the hero's journey comes in. The hero's journey helps explain that the model is ongoing—it's not one-and-done. My experience has shown me that leadership is a long-term game that is never won or lost. The stock markets drive short-termism in organizations. It's fine to set the goal of being the best in the market, but markets give us only a snapshot in time. The art of leadership is to create a sustainable network of systems and habits in others that outlives the leader. Market leadership just happens to be a symptom of robust systems-and-habits-based leadership.

The Pi2 model provides a route map for and provides guidance on how to navigate the challenges that leaders face: determining and maintaining a purpose, recruiting and inspiring a team, energizing and stretching those around them, helping them grow and thrive, and then sustaining that iterative process over time. The model demonstrates how a leader can be more wrong to be successful and learn fast. The journey, if lived with the mindset of being more wrong, is filled with opportunities to fail—sometimes terrifyingly so—and to learn and grow. The rewards are great for you and your clients because the journey delivers long-term, sustainable, and outstanding performance. That's what I have experienced and want to be able to enable in your leadership approach.

The End Result

Have you ever met that person or leader whom you found utterly compelling? These people exude confidence when they walk into a room and in how they deal with anything that is thrown at them. They seem to have a conviction about them that encourages you to trust and want to follow them. They articulate a compelling purpose of why they do what they do. They are very clear about their identity and what they stand for, even if it clashes with a mainstream view. They also have a natural ability to build connection. They are able to adapt their physicality and vocality to show emotion and empathy, no matter the culture, and to build trust and intimacy with people, no matter what happens around them.

We could teach and coach the four styles alone and develop good leaders. Outstanding, compelling leadership, however, is embodied in confidence, conviction, and connection. This can be achieved only when the leaders master the three enablers—purpose, identity, and presence—as mentioned above, so we'll introduce you to those first. Then we will outline the refreshingly direct conversations, systems, and habits that bring them into smooth play with, and embed them in, the four leadership styles.

The Three Enablers

Purpose

In every leader's desire to agitate for the future, there is a journey taken or about to be taken. The leader will act as the guide on that journey. That journey usually has a starting point, and it has a purpose.

In working with leaders and to illustrate the importance and creation of purpose, we set up an apparent exercise, where we hand teams a kit of materials and ask them to build a toy. Typically the work is somewhat sloppy and the thinking behind it is something like, "Well, this is good enough." Halfway through the exercise, however, we play a rather haunting video that connects an abused child to the toy the teams are making. We make clear that their toy is actually being sent to someone like this person in the video, and that it will change that person's life. The exercise has changed and it is at that moment that all the teams shift to a heightened sense of care and engagement.

As Simon Sinek said so well in his 2009 TEDx Talk, "People don't buy what you do; they buy why you do it." The purpose you create and test will lie at the core of every decision and action taken by you as the leader and will remain your and your team's True North. It means having an image of something powerful and a drive to achieve it that will transform life for you and others. An outstanding leader has an inner drive that is fueled by an authentic and personal purpose. This purpose can be arrived at and defined in many different ways (we will look at this in depth in Chapter 3).

As I've said, my purpose is to create a measurable playground to disrupt the way people are led. That drives everything I do, and it is at the heart of the Pi2 model. In my darkest moments, I go back to why I do the things I do. As I lead my team, are we fundamentally pulling together toward disrupting the way people are led? If I am not doing that, then I need to question what I am doing. As I raise my girls, am I creating a playground for them to learn?

Identity

If the purpose is why you do what you do and why people should follow you, then the how you do things is built around the choice of how you want to be known—or what you want to be known for. This is the enabler we call "identity" (covered in more detail in Chapter 4). As a leader, even if you struggle to identify a purpose, it is essential to have a true and authentic identity. Some aspects of our identities are given to us, such as our gender, skin color, and height; some aspects are chosen or taken on. Put simply, I have a choice to cycle or to be a cyclist. I have a choice to mentor or be a mentor. And so with leadership, I can just lead or I can choose to adopt the identity of a leader, and everything that goes with it.

In our work over the last fifteen years, my team and I have worked extensively on the concept of personal branding. Whether we like it or not, we have a brand or a promise that we are "giving off" to people around us. Even when we decide to go for a low profile in a situation, we have made a conscious choice, and that affects others. Therefore, if we desire to be known for something, we need to work at it. For brand, read identity. Our identity is how we choose to present ourselves to the world and how we want to be known.

Presence

When I started my career, I seemed to be able to hold an audience or engage with people in a team with humor and warmth. However, my bosses and colleagues always told me that I needed this magic thing called "gravitas." When I started working with Jacqueline Farrington, she unlocked what that was. It was couched in this thing called presence. Presence (detailed in Chapter 5) comprises the perceived and real impact a leader has on others either through their in-the-moment interactions or via a legacy built up over time.

Your presence is a sign of your ability to be seamlessly agile in adapting your style and approach. This comes only through deep, purposeful practice. The notion that you are born with presence misses the point—you might be born with various elements of it, but to be agile in the full spectrum of presence needs the application of purposeful practice. Your presence is a vital component in your success as a leader. It includes both your level of prominence—how much or how little you are noticed—and your level of gravitas—how (appropriately) light or serious you are in tone and content.

One Conversation at a Time

The enablers are critical to Pi2: they make up the engine that drives the vehicle, and like all engines, it needs to be well oiled to run smoothly. In order to bring the enablers into smooth play with the leadership styles, you need to have conversations—one conversation at a time. Conversations are at the heart of every interaction you have as a leader, whether with one of your boards, the team or individual team members, or customers. They are the oxygen that feeds effective energy in leadership. For these conversations to be effective and powerful, they need to be refreshingly direct. I will explore in greater detail what this means for you in Chapter 6.

Leadership is not a popularity contest in this model. You don't need to be best friends with people; they need to respect and believe in you, and believe that the trust is real between you and them. The levels of respect and trust you earn or command as a leader are fundamentally about how you have the important conversations. You bring your leadership to life with an ability to craft conversations that light fires in bellies—but also under backsides.

Your mandate to lead comes from your team and customers. You need to create an edge, and that requires you to lead with a refreshing approach to your conversations as well as being direct and to the point. Individuals should feel that they can amplify their voice and that they are heard and understood. They need to feel that their truth in any situation is being sought and listened to. The unsaid in conversations needs to be identified and raised so that all the data is present. In this way, the level of your conversations is such that you can achieve outstanding results without worrying that anyone is sensitive to being dealt with in a transparent and direct way. Refreshingly direct is a mindset that when used in conversations drives respect.

Four Leadership Styles

Throughout your journey, you will need to deploy four key styles: Host, Energizer, Disruptor, and Catalyst. Each style has two components. We will look at them in full detail in Chapters 7 through 10. Here's a brief overview.

Host

I've always measured great leaders I have met by the quality of their network—those who work with them, are led by them and then leave with their blessing, keep in contact with them, recommend them, sing their praises, trust them, and want to be part of their human ecosystem. Just as you can tell a lot about a person by their friends, you can tell a lot about a leader by their connections. I have a list of leaders I work with whom I respect, particularly in this context. They have an exceptional network of people around them. But to say there is one that I hold above all others would miss the point. The network of relationships must be active and engaged and each leader and their network face very different situations.

We know that a leader needs followers and followers need a leader. That is a basic premise of leadership. It embraces the leader's need first of all to connect—or, more appropriately, already to have a depth of connection—with a wider team, and, second, to engage with that team so they start to build connection within their group, and with others, on a number of different levels.

When you are a leader, your followers need to connect to your purpose, or True North. That purpose, to be effective, will already be part of who you are and the messages you communicate to your wider connections. Connecting means creating a strong emphasis on unique, interpersonal relationships across a wide variety of personalities, opinions, and beliefs. The goal is to attract a group of people to gather toward a common purpose.

You want your followers to be able to grow to their potential within that journey and purpose. They may be from minority groups who have been overlooked for roles or have struggled to find a voice. They may be strong leaders who have always wanted to achieve in their career without "selling their soul to corporate." They may be people who are looking for a way to reenergize themselves and their teams. Many want to hire fully experienced and developed people, but an organization's true necessity is to learn how to grow its own people. Not only is this cheaper, and not only does it ensure they grow to fit your style, but it is also a huge recruitment attraction when you are known as a developer of people and their careers.

You need to ensure that your team is diverse and inclusive to meet future challenges and the wide range of customer profiles you serve. Diversity and inclusion bring fresh ideas and ways of thinking. One of my consultant friends, Darren Levy, said that there is a need to invite true diversity to the dance; my take is that we also need to ask them to bring their own music, as we can learn so much from it, and ours may be getting a little old. In fact, your connections and followers should also ideally include your customers, and they bring their own music and dances already.

Establishing connections with other people is important, but don't think about it as a numbers game with LinkedIn contacts. It is more about the quality of those connections, their type and depth, and how you as leader engage those you have connected with. You must orchestrate the building of trust within this group of newly forming relationships to the point at which they actively wish to collaborate with each other toward the common purpose for which they joined the group.

More than just "forming, storming, and norming," connecting and engaging means creating a place of psychological safety, where individuals are able to speak up and feel they have enough freedom of expression to be more wrong. That is a tough ask at the best of times. And as your team becomes more diverse, the mix of your followers' different styles and backgrounds can be even more difficult to host. But once engaged, that very diversity will develop into something special and unique that makes your followers, as a force, unstoppable. In his book *Rebel Ideas*, Matthew Syed explores the work on cognitive diversity that is beginning to bring to life the fact that inspiration for decision making comes from true cognitive diversity. To seek and find people who think differently to you as a leader allows you to avoid the trap of only hearing your own thoughts. It also allows you to avoid living in an echo chamber that does not challenge your way of thinking.

Energizer

An inspired and energized team normally has a leader with two characteristics: an ability to craft and tell a compelling story and a strong inner drive and resilience. The compelling story inspires the team to want to have an active part in it (to the point of crafting their own role), and the inner drive and front-foot energy of the leader sustains the followers.

I have had the pleasure of hearing a number of clients' career timelines that they've shared with their people over the years. Two in particular had a big impact on me. The first was that of a client friend, the late Drew Cameron. He was a compelling and inspiring leader in many ways, and he would tell the story of his career with clear examples that illustrated certain points he wanted to make. In my opinion, his biggest strength was bringing people of diverse backgrounds and cultures together and creating a shared story for them all. Drew told of his friend and work colleague Coolasinga, who was the first Sri Lankan to work at the shipyards in Govan, Glasgow. The workers in the shipyards, as a rule, were white—and staunch supporters of Rangers Football Club. It was already tough for Coolasinga to come in as a new person with a different skin color, but he also showed amazing courage being a fan of Celtic Football Club, the archrivals of Rangers, especially when divisions between supporters had strong roots in culture and religion. The fact that he was also a friend of Drew, himself a staunch Rangers supporter, showed Drew's ability to see his friend as inspiration in his own story—that is, he was inspired to bring people from different geographies, religions, and cultures together into his network and see them for themselves, no matter what.

The second career story that struck me was that of my client friend Sarah Garton. I hold her up, as do many women who hear her speak or work with her, as a powerful advocate of people, particularly women. It is not so much what she says as what she has done that brings to life her passion. She is a successful woman who has overcome the challenges of family illness and career highs and lows and yet shows resilience in caring more about others and their stories. Sarah did what is known as "career boomeranging" (leaving and returning to the same organization). The risk she took to go off and challenge herself, learn from the experience, and return to a Fortune Global 500 company with an accelerated pace in her career inspires people—she successfully turned what some might call a mistake into a career enhancer. Sarah's story resonates mainly with women who have struggled in their roles as partner, mother, and businessperson. It was only in the telling of her story that she realized the motivating influence she has on others—which has been reinforced by an award for most inspirational leader.

Both Sarah and Drew enhanced their effect through compelling stories others wanted to live. People consider it an honor to have taken part in their ventures. Such stories as these leaders tell continue to help others see the next stage in the journey toward the purpose that already connects them. At the heart of a leader's compelling story is a place where people believe they can write their own chapter. They see a future where they matter and make a difference. As Energizer, the leader is now taking a step forward and shaping the path for the followers to journey on; they are not only connected but also included.

We use the term "drive" to describe the inner drive of the leader. The old view of the leader ordering and driving their people to charge into battle is not sustainable in the fast-moving world we live in. Nor is it in line with the concept of the leader as the guide who shapes a path for the followers. Drive, like purpose, is a source of energy.

How can leaders maintain their levels of energy, purpose, and passion, and transfer that energy to their followers? The leader must take responsibility and be "properly selfish" to ensure they remain fit to lead—taking time to replenish themselves mentally (for example, through meditation) and physically (with exercise, nutrition, and sleep). You could argue that there is also a need for a spiritual side to this—not necessarily religious, but an inner drive based on values and beliefs. This can be seen in identity as well, and both identity and purpose can fuel the levels of inner drive. In nourishing that inner drive, you are also role-modeling it as a requirement for your team. It stands you both in good stead for the challenges ahead.

This area of leadership with drive has been given renewed focus in recent years. The burnout of leaders has manifested itself in disillusion, life traumas, or reliance on outside stimulants that cause their own problems. Just like managing an engine in a highly tuned car, the leader needs to be aware of their physical and mental systems and learn how to manage them effectively. The work on health does not start when injury or illness happens; it starts by being proactive and finding the right balances of fuel, oxygen, and heat in your life to keep your fire burning. I am lucky that I have many people who inspire me in this area. My COO, Sharon Hardcastle, has a healthy life that is based on exercise in the form of power walking. Traveling with Sharon in our work together leads me to walk with her in the mornings. Our record was 21 miles around Manhattan in the heat and humidity. She also knows what she needs, such as how much sleep and—an important part when it comes to drive—fun and enjoying a night out with friends to recharge.

Disruptor

The demands of the market, its regulators, and global growth, and the changing needs of customers mean standing still is not an option for an organization or any team, no matter what industry they are in. Since leadership means agitating for the future, leaders need to find ways to disrupt the way they think and work before others do it for them. They also should be constantly refreshing their followers' outlook.

It is ironic that most leaders wanting to learn about leadership choose to attend a Leadership 101 training course to be perfect as leaders. As a provider of that kind of training, my first piece of guidance for leaders is to get out from behind their desk and just spend time with their people and their customers, observing and being curious. To make a ding in the universe, as Steve Jobs said, we need to go out and create a playground. Understanding our customers and being empathetic in our approach, we can bring fresh views and ideas—a wow factor to how we operate and deliver. We can make changes and bring difference without attending a leadership course, just by doing this simple thing.

The leader as Disruptor has two main responsibilities: to experiment and challenge.

It is no longer just the role of research and development departments to experiment. The world is changing: people are investing by crowd-funding in ideas before they become products. The belief that if you are proud of your product, you are too late to market speaks to getting your offerings out early and often to customers, and using this process as an opportunity to learn while you build—in other words, "build to think." Experimenting means that, using feedback and insights you've gained while releasing products and developing, you constantly make small, incremental changes (in habits or products) internally, before there is bigger disruption by external forces. Prototyping gives an edge to your team and customers—you can evaluate and refine and move forward. What you're doing is taking your team on rougher seas to stretch and challenge them. By failing fast through testing and experimenting, like regularly ingesting little bits of poison, to use Nassim Nicholas Taleb's metaphor in his aforementioned book *Antifragile*, you and your team can build up a resistance, become antifragile, and develop an edge that keeps freshness in your products and approaches.

The responsibility to challenge relies on information. This information can be quantitative, qualitative, or a mixture of both, and it comes from many different sources. The data from the wider world, your team, you, and your clients can be overwhelming, but you need that data to create insights and make tough decisions through effectively challenging what is and is not working. Data is becoming so important that there are specialist organizations that help you calculate the value of data for your balance sheet. Chief data officers are being recruited to provide "dropdown insights" in real time to help leaders and their teams in agile decision making—just like fighter pilots have in their visors while they fly.

The measurement system of leadership is aided by technology and machine learning, but the leader also still needs to have the refreshingly direct conversations that occur on the back end of the data being produced and the insights derived. Asking the right questions and debating the right insights around real, and live, data is now an agile and robust business tool. That data means even more when your customers are the ones giving you live feedback and information on your ideas, products, and services. The fact is that, like sports teams' managers and coaches, leaders are measuring everything that impacts their teams: their motivation, happiness, inner drive, resilience, passion, attitude—not as a policing tool but so they can see their effectiveness and make changes when necessary. This is also what I mean by "a measurable playground": we need to know and understand what we're gaining—and losing—from our play.

Catalyst

The more challenging situations a leader and their team take on, the more the leader needs their team members to be growing their skills and capability. The development of capability is, in my view, always up to the individuals. However, as a leader you have a responsibility to develop systems and habits that enhance the learning and development of your team members. Leadership is both reflective and developmental in nature and embodies the dual roles of mentor and coach.

Mentoring is making a big comeback (if it ever really went away). The reason for this is that organizations have identified that they have collective wisdom, from the top to the bottom and across functions and divisions, and it needs to be shared. Providing mentoring systems is one way of enabling this to happen.

So what is mentoring? There are many definitions. The key expressions included in the definitions of mentoring have elements about the mentor—supportive, caring, has experience, knowledge, or wisdom the mentee does not have. They have descriptions about the relationship itself—learning, sharing of knowledge, experience, wisdom, exchange, conversation (not a download from the mentor). They also have descriptions of the mentee—willing and ready individual, ready to have this exchange of knowledge, experience, and wisdom, on a journey and needing help. Caring is an important part of the package. Mentors create their ability to mentor effectively through their experience of pain points in their lives and how they have overcome them. The fact that I have been made redundant, for instance, gives me a pain point I have dealt with; crafting a point of view on how I dealt with this helps me guide others to deal with or avoid the situation in their lives.

Pain points vary, from being fired to hating your boss, to dealing with a toxic culture, to overcoming burnout, to having successfully built long-term client relationships through hardship. Having been through difficult experiences, the mentor becomes a guide for their mentees and network. They offer advice that is up to the mentee to accept, reject, or modify. By sharing these teachable points of view, mentors build capability in others.

Leaders, too, need a range of mentors for their own hero's journey. Every leader needs outside perspectives that can guide wisdom in their decisions and how they work with their team. And in role-modeling that need, leaders set a great tone for the team to see mentors as a core part of what they, too, need.

Coaching has been a desired skill for leaders for many years now. The fact that it is not universally lived as a skill says a lot about how it has been taught, or perceived, in the past. Sir John Whitmore is known as the pioneer of executive coaching. His definition of coaching includes unlocking people's potential, maximizing their performance, and helping them learn, not just telling or teaching them what they need to know. Whitmore's *Coaching for Performance* was one of the first books I read in my work in this field. It still resonates today. However, I now prefer the excellent book *The Coaching Habit* by Michael Bungay Stanier, a good friend and a great writer. He talks about how to be a bit more coachlike and a bit more curious, and how to coach in ten minutes or less. His approach is conversational, and I find myself using his questions on a regular basis to make my coaching more informal and engaging.

Coaching is about building capability in others by unlocking their personal potential through conversations in which you are questioning, prompting, allowing self-reflection, and letting the individual do some reframing. This coaching style also brings in the power of using silence to do the heavy lifting in the conversation. It sounds simple when you start with an obvious question like "What's on your mind?" It is more difficult to maintain, however, and we will cover that further later.

The Essential Tension

That's a brief introduction to the four styles of leadership that make up Pi2: Host, Energizer, Disruptor, and Catalyst. Chapters 7 through 10 will show you about them in more detail and teach you how to realize them in yourself.

Two further points need to be made clear. First, there is an explicit tension built into each of the four styles and its twin elements—connect and engage; inspire and drive; experiment and challenge; mentor and coach. This tension fuels the success of the model by fostering an often uncomfortable but always creative edge. The tension needs to be carefully managed but it contributes to the richness of the model. Second, the right-hand quadrants of the model—Energizer and Disruptor—emphasize action by the leader and focus on forward motion toward the purpose, while the left-hand quadrants—Catalyst and Host—emphasize planning and reflection and building a mandate from the team. Each emphasis has its time and place, but the model is a cogent, living, iterative whole designed to measure and improve your performance and, in doing so, expand your scope to be more wrong.

Is it easy? No. Is it hard work? Yes. Will it take courage and resilience? Yes. Is it worth it? Yes. Do I role-model it every day in my working life? ... No. So how do I describe the thrill and excitement of Pi2 in action?

The Pi2 Experience

The analogy that works best for me is of a TOPGUN pilot controlling a multimillion-dollar plane flying at the speed of sound, making adjustments and decisions at speed. That pilot has honed their understanding of the possibilities of that combination of plane, pilot, and situations through rigorous and purposeful practice in different elements and pitching themselves against the "best of the best." In the US Navy Strike Fighter Tactics Instructor program, also known as the TOPGUN program, they have many hours of practice. Each hour is followed by analysis—in some cases, ten hours of analysis for one hour of flying or "dogfights." I met a woman whose son is a TOPGUN instructor. I could have sat and listened for hours to the stories of her son's training. In the air, they don't have the chance to stop. They hardwire instinct through hours of purposeful practice, creating habits and systems for in-the-moment top performance.

In real time, those pilots have an in-helmet visor that provides them with an overview of their ecosystem. Our Pi2 Leadership Assessment provides that kind of thing for leaders, with a pulse element that gives them an ongoing score for their leadership ecosystem. Think about it in the context of a Net Promoter Score. The simple question behind the Net Promoter Score is: "Would you recommend this person, service, or company to others?" The Pi2 has that scoring embedded in it as a summary score for the leader: "Would you recommend this person as a leader?"

For the leader to strive to be more wrong and improve their Net Promoter Score requires a "visor screen" that projects the real-time readouts on the leader's systems. The ecosystem of the leader is made up of a number of different elements that impact each other in multiple and nonlinear ways. The recruitment of a new team member or follower affects the levels of risk-taking in the wider group. The loss of a team member has the same effect. The gain or loss of a customer impacts the wider group. Likewise for the following: the change of direction required for a new product or to react to a new customer, a new regulatory requirement, a market downturn or upturn. The leader must be engaged and able to work with their followers to adjust to the new forces in an agile way. They first need to be able to measure the health of that ecosystem. They are able to do this through the use of the Pi2 model.

It is also not just about reacting to change. In fact, the healthier principle behind "be more wrong" is to disrupt yourself, your ecosystem, and your followers continually, before others do. In doing that, it is about being innovative, insightful, and purposeful in order to develop foresight—the ability to prepare for changes that have not already happened. It is difficult to do, but in shaping markets and trends, organizations are able to fend off external challenges.

The clinching element for me of combining the ethos of being more wrong and the hero's journey with the thinking on systems and habits is that the Pi2 model has embedded in it the purpose of guiding and supporting your team members to be heroes for themselves. By creating an effective ecosystem, you will enhance your team's resilience and desire to embrace the change that is constant in all aspects of our lives.

But all of this depends on the ongoing development of robust habits and systems that sustain you on your journey of being more wrong.

systems and habits: the secret sauce

M Y VIEWS ON how to live my life and lead have been transformed by a simple piece of writing by James Clear in *Atomic Habits*: "You do not rise to the level of your goals. You fall to the level of your systems."

I have bad habits in abundance. My approach for dealing with them, until recently, was to berate myself for not having better habits. We all have bad habits we want to break and good habits we want to adopt. Every year many of us make New Year's resolutions—some of us make the same one every year, since we never keep it. When I conduct workshops, I ask attendees to write down certain actions and outcomes and to keep track of their progress when they leave the workshop. Most of them last seven days, if that. It was only when I read *Atomic Habits* that I suddenly had a revelation: the problem is not about my goals to change habits; it is about the systems that I have, filled with habits.

Working hard is good. As Dwayne "The Rock" Johnson says, "Be the hardest worker in the room." Just don't be that person who works hard on only one area in the gym. We need systems to ensure that our hard work embodies habits and actions that bring about sustainable change. Johnson has a focused training pattern for his gym work. He has fueling systems to ensure that he has energy for those workouts. He also has "cheat days" on which he eats three huge pizzas, or burgers, to make sure that he mentally feeds the fact that it is about rewards as well. He is also focused on his systems that allow his work to fail forward toward his purpose. He has his film career that he delivers on in a focused way, playing the same character most of the time and playing on his physique. He is committed to his family, and he highlights his time with them in his schedule. He has his roots in Samoa and the Samoan culture. His systems are set up for him to be his best self.

Similarly, the systems we have as leaders need to be set up to allow us to be our best selves. We need to ensure we are clear on our purpose and we constantly revisit our story. We need to have a system based on our identity, with measures to ensure that we are portraying—and others are experiencing—the identity we want others to experience. We want to have our systems set up with habits that strengthen our physicality and vocality so we can be agile in—to use Darren Levy's metaphor again—dancing with the music and people we choose to dance with. We want to have systems that increase the desire of the right people to connect with us. We want systems in place that allow those followers, once connected, including our customers, to be able to amplify their voice and feel psychologically safe to share their concerns and ideas. We need systems in place to allow us to craft, tell, and constantly recast our story that inspires others. We need systems to ensure that our personal drive is strong and sustained to deal with the challenges that arise. We need systems, full of habits, practice, and feedback loops, that encourage us to experiment and create an edge in our work and also allow us to make tough decisions when ideas fail and we have to kill them off. We need systems, full of habits, practice, and feedback loops, to develop the capability and alignment of our followers to then go on and confidently risk failing again—being more wrong, and then more wrong again.

We also have to work out what habits and practice are going to fuel those systems so we are successful. We need our workouts planned and systematized so that we achieve balanced growth as a leader. In all of my work as a coach, I have learned the hard lesson that one coaching session or one program is not enough to change behavior. In fact, a lifetime of coaching and programs is not enough. The only way that sustainable leadership change is possible is by a systematic overhaul of the systems and habits through which a leader operates. Then it is about purposeful practice and measurement of these systems and habits. "Not only is practice necessary to art, it is art," Stephen Nachmanovitch says in his book *Free Play*. The art of leadership, and the core of *Be More Wrong*, is that all of these systems and habits need practice. You are both the role model and the coach for your followers as they develop appropriate systems and habits for themselves—through practice.

Leaders often naturally default to the things that they do well or that have served them well in the past—for example, the sales leader always goes to the sales conversation that got them where they are now. But that does not necessarily make us successful here, where we are now leaders. In my early leadership years, I was good at "winging it with integrity," so that's what I did. But this approach did not work for everybody, or it required me to be involved in everything—always an issue when a leader should be getting out of their team's way. Even today, in the Pi2 model, I feel at my very best when playing to an audience, presenting to a group, getting buy-in to a way forward—in Pi2 terms, engaging and inspiring. These skills feed my need to tell stories and engage others. However, doing this without focus on other areas leads to the equivalent of that person in the gym with a great upper body and no leg strength to support it; risking the mandate I need with my followers for the sake of a good story. So I need to understand the systems and habits that will keep each area of the model healthy and growing—whether or not they're where I want to play or feel at home.

Naturally, any time we explore a new area or have to improve, it takes experimenting and hard work. As I started my yoga practice, for instance, I was an inflexible man, someone who had done plenty of running but very little stretching. To become flexible and strong throughout my body was going to take some time—a lifetime, in fact, because there's always more to gain ... and without keeping it up, I will get stiffer and weaker again. If we have a finite mindset when developing something like flexibility, the measures are arbitrary and become meaningless. If we adopt the mindset that systems and habits of practice are needed each day for our lifetime—an infinite mindset—then we will enjoy long-term success.

The Pi2 model has ideas of the systems and habits needed for leaders built into it. You might like the ones in the book; you might need to find ones that fit you better. The list I present here is not exhaustive. It is an exploration of the tensions in the systems that leaders need to develop—the need to be "properly selfish" to sustain your personal sources of drive to allow you as a leader to spend that energy in being more wrong and sailing in rougher seas. The tension of needing to pump energy into your relationships with your followers to allow you to risk that energy as they face failure and challenges. The tension of knowing the right balance of lighting fires in bellies and under backsides to get buy-in and also get movement and action. All of these inherent tensions provide a living, breathing system of leadership to keep you balanced and more effective as a leader.

We will look at specific systems and habits in the context of each of the individual styles of leadership, but there are also broad systems and habits that will support your leadership, and I will set some of them out here in this chapter. I know from experience that some habits are easier than others to form and that almost all are easily lost in changing circumstances. And embedding new habits, even if we perceive their value, can be a challenge to the best of us. The COVID-19 pandemic certainly brought that lesson home.

As you read this book, it will become clear to you that the biggest influencers on my thinking are Amy Edmondson and her work on psychological safety and James Clear and his book *Atomic Habits*. Of equal influence are the habits of creative people encouraged by Design Thinking from ExperiencePoint and IDEO. It is worth spending a bit of time now on a brief run-through of Design Thinking specifically—that is, its habits and the needs of that system to be successful.

Design Thinking

Five years ago, I was talking to one of our South African consultants, Brad Shorkend. He was working with a start-up business incubator in South Africa, and he was singing the praises of a company called ExperiencePoint. ExperiencePoint had partnered with IDEO to create powerful simulations to bring Design Thinking to life. It was a system that transformed the way start-ups think. I had been screwing up most of my career yet was somehow successful, and, before I knew it, somebody—Andrew Webster of ExperiencePoint—was sitting in front of me and telling me that making mistakes was now cool. By conducting small low-risk experiments and learning fast from them, you could be successful. I had to learn how this works and develop the habits of doing it.

Here is what I learned.

The Six Habits of Creative People

Habit 1: Frame a problem with a "How might we...?" question. Frame your question so that you identify the right problem. Every time you come across a challenge that is complex (one without an obvious solution), meaningful (any progress would have a disproportionate impact), and human-centric (people's behaviors drive outcomes), there is a place for Design Thinking. "How might we...?" is a good question because it is not as limited as a simple "How do we...?" and it encourages a growth mindset.

Habit 2: Gather inspiration. Inspire new thinking by observing, without judgment, to discover what people really need. This is one of my favorite habits of Design Thinking. It allows you to break free from the shackles of how you have always worked. Take your "How might we...?" and add observation, and you will find what people care about, workarounds, adaptations, and surprises. These are the criteria of great observations. Get out from behind your desk, go observe your users, and see what you see and what they tell you.

Habit 3: Synthesize for action. Make meaning out of the diverse information you gather through your observation to identify a focus. This means joining the dots of your observations to create insights. The criteria for great insights are that they are authentic (based on real observations), revealing (identifying something that we have not seen before), and nonobvious (for example, if you phoned a friend, they would say, "Wow, I never thought of that").

Habit 4: Generate ideas. Push past obvious solutions to come up with breakthrough ideas. The main method of doing this is brain-storming, generating in a focused way as many ideas as possible on a focused topic. It stimulates creativity and innovation.

Habit 5: Make ideas tangible. Build rough representations of your ideas to help you think. This means getting out and testing your ideas quickly. The concept that we should "build to think," meaning just being focused on bringing the idea to life, is liberating. Just getting the ideas out allows you to then evaluate, edit, and improve or move on. This is how you get to the good stuff. There are many ways to do this. The aim is to also allow you to involve other people with your ideas quickly and shape better ideas at a very early stage. As I mentioned earlier, if your idea is perfect, it is too late to market. Fail ugly and early!

Habit 6: Test to learn. Experiment your way to market through iterative prototyping of your ideas to test key behaviors of people. These experiments are critical to test levels of user experience. Experiments can also kill off an idea very quickly. Here, the value of being more wrong becomes more tangible: less time and money are wasted in the drawn-out development of something that any one of these habits could have revealed as a nonstarter. Just imagine, therefore, what the value will be in the ideas that fly.

THE EMBEDDING of these six habits into what we called Design House allowed my team and me to start to work with our clients in a different way. The system needed to be fed and maintained with new clients willing to be part of the playground, new partners bringing new ways of doing things, new team members who had a growth mindset to see failure as fun, and, finally, a new form of leadership, in which I left my ego and expertise at the door and immersed myself in the thoughts and ideas of others.

Embedding Habits and Systems

Each habit has, as Charles Duhigg points out in his book *The Power of Habit*, three stages: a trigger, a behavior, and a reward. We know that we should have more good habits and change or eliminate bad habits, but how do we do this? How do we recognize the trigger? How do we change the behavior that greets the trigger? And in some cases, how do we change the reward? My response to all of this has been to develop and use what I call "purposeful practice."

The principle of purposeful practice was initially established as the concept of deliberate practice. It was brought to fame by Malcolm Gladwell in his book *Outliers*. James Clear describes deliberate practice as "a special type of practice that is purposeful and systematic. While regular practice might include mindless repetitions, deliberate practice requires focused attention and is conducted with the specific goal of improving performance." It is the breaking down of a skill and deliberately practicing those smaller pieces of that skill again and again to improve performance. Each time you practice, however, you expose yourself to getting it wrong—to being wrong. This exposure is essential for experimenting and failing fast and forward.

The world of tennis has been blessed in the last ten years to have three or four amazing talents playing at the same time. In another era, Andy Murray might have been adding to his Grand Slams, but the fact that Djokovic, Nadal, and Federer are around has stopped him. Murray is seen as one of the hardest trainers working on all aspects of his game, but facing Djokovic, Nadal, and Federer, he

has an added challenge in that all of them have also been applying purposeful practice to their disciplines. They continually break
down their game into habits and apply purposeful practice to all of
the elements in order to build a balanced, effective approach and,
above all, a winning game. The harder you work and practice, the
luckier you will get, as pro golfer Gary Player once said. Likewise,
the breaking down of leadership into habits and purposefully practicing them is how you grow. And it is the constant, unrelenting
purposeful practice that will hone your abilities and ultimately win
the game, set, match, and championship.

The greatest challenge of purposeful practice is to remain
focused. In the beginning, it is showing up and doing repetitions.
This repetition carries the risk of carelessness, overlooking small
errors, and missing frequent opportunities for improvement.
However, by remaining focused and practicing for improvement,
we exploit the natural tendency of the human brain to transform
repeated behaviors into automatic habits.

Nesting Habits

When I first started using the Headspace app and meditating, I
struggled to maintain the habit and discipline. Finding twenty minutes for sitting in a weird upright position, with my hands on my
thighs, was tricky. My answer was to start Headspace immediately
after a walk or a 5:15 morning workout. Now, having nested those
two habits together, I add a third, fourth, and even fifth habit. After
my workout and Headspace, I now do a process to help a problem
with my eyes (a heated eye beanbag). While I do this lying on my
back on the floor, I add ten minutes of Pilates. And most recently,
during a COVID-19 lockdown, I have started to listen to ten minutes of new music or music I have not listened to for a while. So I
build and maintain five good habits by nesting them into a routine.
They are all feeding the system of personal drive: the Headspace
practice feeds my mental health and clears my mind; the exercise

fuels my energy and health; the eye process ensures my eyes are healthy; the Pilates strengthens my core; the music, as somebody once said, fuels my soul.

This nesting of habits, as James Clear calls it, allows me to have recovery time from exercise (giving my body twenty minutes of relaxation to recover from exhaustion is a blessed relief!) while finding a way to work out mentally as well. As a new discipline, and with purposeful practice, I now see the early start, workout, and Headspace (plus the other habits) as a reward—my space and quiet time. So, really, it nests as 1) early start, 2) exercise, 3) Headspace, plus..., plus... I can also see the early start as the trigger, the workout as the behavior, and the twenty minutes of clearing my mind as the reward. The longer-term benefits of the nested habits now are core strength, weight loss, better thought processes, and healthier eyes. The music has been a bonus and has actually reconnected me with a couple of friends, Jack Bailey and Kevin Allinson, who share my love of music.

I model this habit nesting in my business as well. I now see my leadership of the business as living a series of purposeful actions, habits, and systems that will drive action in my team—from taking the time to write this book, to spending sixty minutes of my day, after exercise and Headspace, with a coffee planning the day ahead, to writing mind maps for programs or coaching sessions no matter how many times I have delivered them. Those habits and drive will allow me to lead the team and myself in deep practice. I am also modeling the habits I want to see in my fully engaged team.

Adapting Habits and Systems to Fit

It is important to choose the right habits. As leaders and individuals, we need to ensure that the habits and systems we adopt fit our purpose, identity, and the presence we want to live. They also need to match the current reality the leader faces. As I write these words, the COVID-19 pandemic rages on. My world and the world all around me has been thrown up in the air. What systems and habits I now have need to fit a different world. I need to adjust, and that means that my systems and habits need to adjust as well—and quickly. The adjustments we all need to make are not always smooth or painless. But the need for these habits and systems and the purposeful practice that supports and embeds them has not changed. How you achieve it all, however, probably has.

Not being able to travel, for example, is a basic adjustment that directly affects my impact as a leader. Whereas before I could energize others in person, now I need to energize others virtually. Experimenting needs to be done virtually, and that requires different systems and habits developed around the use of unfamiliar tools. The changes have benefits in some ways: less commuting, more time with the family, and more exercise time. But being cut off from others physically requires me to embed habits around phone calls, note taking, and even redefining what I understand of my boundaries with others (how real but falsely disconcerting it feels when someone in a location miles away can intrude on your personal space by sitting too close to their camera!).

The new way of the world has also affected my habit of getting up at 5:15 and working out to start my day. Working from home, I am now finding that my energy levels are low at about 2:00 in the afternoon. My choices of new habits to counter this are to either have a power nap at 2:00 or change my exercise time. My nesting of habits meant I would work out, then do Headspace, then complete my habit tracker over coffee. Now I have shifted to working out at lunchtime to reenergize myself for the afternoon. This means my habit "nest" has been disrupted, and I am forming and embedding new habits. But I fully expect to be more wrong on the way before I find what is right for me and the moment!

The systems we have as leaders are in some ways clearer as a result of the pandemic disruption. The Host systems of networking and psychological safety come into play early. The communication and resilience systems of the Energizer role are clearer and need some real work. The systems of Design Thinking and decision making are now on platforms that are still a bit clunky for us as we practice their use as Disruptors. The coaching and mentoring systems for our team are harder in some ways in that our daily connections in the office do not exist. However, in other ways, we are creating new systems for them by going back to regular telephone calls and written notes, helping us to be clear about expectations.

Within all of these systems—and there are many more—we have to start building habits that enable each system to be self-sustaining. Our networking system at Potential Squared used to be based on the ability to just drop in and see clients with no agenda while we were in London. We were able to take over a whiteboard and shape some thinking or new ideas. Now we have a visual interface created by Zoom or Microsoft Teams that needs to be mastered, and we have to create new habits to make these platforms work for us. We now have to realize that our clients and network contacts are feeling Zoomed out and need a fresh approach. We have to create new habits to share information and ideas. Drafting ideas on PowerPoint, making hand-drawn sketches, taking polls, and sharing data are now an extra nested habit on top of just keeping in contact. We need to explore online platforms like Slack for project communication and Miro for collaboration. The new world is forcing us to move into experimenting and trying new ways of engaging.

This book will go further into habits and systems that support each style and enabler of Pi2 and will provide examples that you can adapt for yourself. But for the moment, here are some of my favorite personal habits for each leadership style:

- **Host:** Pay it forward. Reach out each week to give something to others without expecting something in return.

- **Energizer:** Do Headspace each day to clear my mind.

- **Disruptor:** Create an advisory board and give them permission to challenge the hell out of me.

- **Catalyst:** Have simple weekly one-to-one meetings where the agenda is set by the other person—to do this, kick off with "What's on your mind?"

How do I keep track of these habits? That is easy: I formed yet another habit—I do a daily habit tracker session with my coffee—after Headspace.

TAKING THE Pi2 Leadership Assessment, which Potential Squared offers, is a good place to start in identifying where your systems and habits as a leader are strong and where they might need attention. The rest of this book takes you on a journey to discover how you can build your capability and scores in all areas of the model. So . . . you start here!

Part Two

the three enablers

3

purpose

THE IMPACT OF TED Talks on the world has been amazing. Earlier, I mentioned one of the most famous talks, given by Simon Sinek in 2009. For me, the most powerful thing he says in it is: "People don't buy what you do; they buy why you do it."

It's a weird thought that you might have a goal that drives you every day of your life—and yet you never achieve it. Imagine you are a general manager of one of the top hotels in the world, Claridge's, and you hold a purpose of achieving "perfection." How do you feel knowing that if you ever think you have achieved your purpose, you have failed? Perfection is in the eye of the beholder and changes for every guest, which means that you can never reach that state for the whole wide range of guests. Perfection was the purpose held by Thomas Kochs—he still holds it now in his role at the Corinthia in London. He is an amazing character and a great leader.

The realization that your guiding purpose is an "infinite game," as Simon Sinek puts it, can be depressing if you hold a finite mindset. But once you realize, as a leader, that people follow you because of why you do something and not what you do or how you do it, it can be a liberating thing. It means that if you get up each day driven by a strong purpose and are clearly articulating a why, then people will follow you and want to be part of your story, even if—or especially because—it has no end.

In fact, my guiding light is not just my purpose of creating a measurable playground to disrupt the way people are led; it's the fact that if I ever think I have fully achieved it, then I have missed the point. That guides and informs everything my team and I do. In our best moments, it is what we celebrate; in our moments of darkness, it is the light that keeps us going.

In the past, being a leader has been about management practice, coaching, team building, and creating a vision—a simple picture of what the future looks like. Now we know it takes more. Yes, you can do very well as a leader with the how and the what in place. But to be outstanding as a leader, the why needs to be compelling and attractive to others. And because the journey is excitingly never-ending, there is a pleasurable moment when you realize that the way to live it is in the moment and focused on creating and experimenting with a network of systems and habits. Those systems and habits, combined with leading indicators to track direction, keep you on course to achieve your infinite-minded purpose. This purpose will lie at the core of every decision and action made by you as the leader and will remain your and your team's True North.

In the Pi2 model, our definition of purpose is: "Having an image, feeling, and set of ideals about why you do what you do. That purpose should have an impact on the transformation of your life and the lives of others. An outstanding leader has an inner drive that is fueled by an authentic and personal purpose."

And this does not mean your values. Yes, your values influence your purpose, but they are just one of the lenses you use to select your purpose. Your purpose must be something that makes you spring out of bed in the morning. It must keep you motivated and energized when all around you energy is being wasted by many distractions and stresses. Your purpose must fuel not only you but also every one of your followers.

I truly believe that anyone can lead. Being a leader isn't a role one is born into. And you can lead without a purpose. In fact, you can even be a good leader without a compelling, authentic purpose. But to be an exceptional and outstanding leader, you need a compelling purpose. Like Martin Luther King Jr., you might have a dream of something better and the drive to pursue it—his was pretty significant and had strong passion behind it. Or, like Richard Branson, your dream might be "to have fun in [my] journey through life and learn from [my] mistakes." For him, this translated into the Virgin Atlantic purpose: "to embrace the human spirit and let it fly." How to nest your purpose as a leader into your businesses is a skill.

With this purpose driving them, leaders can experiment, fail early and often, learn fast, and achieve great things. What this means is that it doesn't matter who you are or how "unlikely" a leader you consider yourself to be. If you care enough to change something in the world, you can lead.

In terms of the Pi2 model, there are many different ways to arrive at and define your purpose. We'll be looking at several.

How I Found My Purpose

The story of my purpose and how I landed on it is like that of many others. It is a series of happenings that did not seem to be linked until I created the final statement. I remember sitting in a conference full of our competitors in the learning and development field. The conference's purpose was to bring together like organizations so that they might learn from each other about how to grow and be more successful. The speaker that day was Josh Bersin of Bersin by Deloitte, and he was saying that human resources, and the learning profession that we represented, needed a significant makeover. He was looking at us in the room as the key people to be part of bringing that makeover to reality. It created a seed of an idea in my mind. It was a bit like in the movie *Field of Dreams* with Kevin Costner, where he builds a baseball field to be reconnected with the ghost of his father: I suddenly had a vision of all of us in the room coming together to build a collaborative way of disrupting how we did learning and development. In other words, as the voice in the film said, if we build it, they will come.

If you've seen the movie, you know how receptive people were to the idea at first. It was amazing how many people in that room did not buy into what I was "selling." I was passionate to the point of being annoying. I suddenly realized that, like the brother-in-law in *Field of Dreams*, they thought I was crazy—"You will lose the farm. Think of your family." But did it discourage me?

Yes! It did! The room was focused on the what and how. They had their own way of doing things and, by many measures, they were more successful than I was. I left that conference feeling slightly discouraged and having mentally placed that idea back into the laboratory. The idea would need new heat added to it to rekindle it.

After three years of experimenting in my mind and actions, the idea popped back onto the front burner. The concept of learning fast was catching on and a series of partners and clients wanted to play with us to create something new. Then the purpose was back on the map, and it has since become our True North. The three years of experimenting and failure stories made me even more determined that our purpose was right. But I would have to build it in order for the rest of the room at the conference to get it and want to play.

So what happened specifically in those three years to bring my idea back to the front of our business? Life. As is often said, "Life is what happens to you while you're busy making other plans." My focus was on driving the existing business. I started to consciously and subconsciously experiment with new products such as Design Thinking and learning experience platforms. Consciously, I knew I had the seed of something, and it also coincided with me starting to write this book. It was amazing how writing a book called *Be More Wrong* and living its ethos in how I ran the business started to make changes.

I was gathering stories that reinforced my passion for my purpose. Stories are the source of learning. When I started to reach out to others in the industry and wider, they told me their stories. I began to go back over my life and career and crystallize learning from what had been my favorite stories to be part of and tell: The fact that I changed my room around every two weeks, as I found I got bored. The fact that I had multiple groups of friends that I got on well with, but when I tried to bring them together, I found that they did not jell. Why was that? I found wonder in reasoning why that had happened. I was creating experiments using the chemistry of people. I was also passionate about the sense of belonging and the concept of the functional family. What did it take to make a functional family? It certainly was not the boring family that never seemed to argue or challenge each other. I found my happiest moments in the creation of energy in parties that were boring or lacked spark. I found the weirdest happiness in proving my father and grandfather wrong: success was not just being able to memorize and recite "Tam o' Shanter" by Robert Burns (which I failed at spectacularly!). All of these stories were rich with data. But as the saying goes, you can't tickle yourself, and it took a glass of wine and a nice grilling from my colleague Jacqueline Farrington to crystallize my first purpose: "to create heroes of the people I work with."

I started to seek out learning partners in clients and colleagues to shape my favorite stories and test out my new purpose. By doing that and all of the above, the habits and systems of the business and my leadership changed, in many ways without me realizing it. Even now, to realize how far we have come, it takes the three times a year when we meet our advisory board and we have to recount what we have done. After three years, the business conditions with the rise of digital learning and the change in delivery methods for learning made the adoption of the new purpose right. We were ready to sail our ship out of the harbor and already had a number of the habits and mindsets necessary to play well on the high seas.

All great stories of heroes (male and female) start with a call to adventure: Frodo in *The Lord of the Rings* assumes the task of carrying the One Ring; Martin Luther King Jr. champions the cause of an end to racism and the introduction of civil and economic rights; my mother took on the purpose of raising three children while holding down two jobs, becoming a top salesperson in medical sales and supporting my father, who was working as a pediatric cardiologist to save babies' lives. For all the different types of leaders we work with—even those who don't know they are a leader yet—there is a call to adventure. That conference I mentioned provided my call to adventure. The adventure was fueled by so much more, but the fire was lit in that room.

Creating Your Own Call to Adventure

Learning how to create your own call to adventure, your own purpose, could be a book in itself.

For those who are given the call to adventure by accident or by a horrible tragedy, the process is clearer. Martin Bromiley took his wife, Elaine, for a routine operation. Due to clinical errors, she died. Martin's resultant quest to ensure the medical profession learned from the death of his wife became his purpose, which has led to a whole new operations culture and new surgical procedures. Martin found his purpose during tragic circumstances. The suffragettes found theirs through injustice: in pain and anger, they sought rights for women.

But if we don't have a negative experience that provides us with our purpose, how do we craft ours?

For some (as it was for me), their purpose is founded on a career of seeing people being led in way that is not exciting or inspiring and those leaders being rewarded for doing an average job. The majority of them would have found their career even more rewarding if they could have created their own playground and had had the opportunity to be more wrong, and that is an incentive for me. My light bulb moment came during the conference I mentioned above. I had been collecting the data and insights for many years. I just needed something to light it—and then to work hard and experiment.

I often compare leadership to lighting fires in bellies and under backsides. When starting to write this book, I looked at the concept of fire. *What do you need to light a fire?* I asked myself. A spark, oxygen, and fuel, I thought, as many people would. And then I spent a long time looking for the spark. Wrongly. Because that's not quite it, is it? It is heat, oxygen, and fuel. The heat already exists, and to cause fire, we just need to create the right conditions. The call to adventure moment is about kindling the heat that already exists in you and others around you. The moments can be given to us, or we can choose to take them.

And purpose can evolve. For almost five years, I wanted "to create heroes of the people I work with." I still do, but that is no longer my True North. The light bulb moment in the conference about the positive role that disruption can play in business has transformed my—and my team's—business purpose into "creating a measurable playground to disrupt the way people are led." And in making this my True North, I am still facilitating the creation of individual heroes.

But light bulb moments, great ideas, and transformational purposes aren't always found by hunting and striving. They often appear at the most unlikely moments, and they aren't always externally prompted. It's only when you become aware that often your best ideas come to you when your mind is switched off—on a run or in the shower, for instance—that you realize we all have the power and the ideas inside ourselves. We just need to fall out of our own thinking. As Jamie Smart writes, using his "inside-out" concept, we can move to inspired action through being able to switch off the interference and turbulence in our minds.

Remember our drunk man looking for keys under a streetlight? His lesson applies here: so many times we seek answers from other sources because "the light seems better," when all the answers we need are within us. Our thinking is just cluttered or frozen. It is the same for purpose. Other peoples' ideas are not a true source of your purpose, and the glare from their ideas can often blind you to your own. It doesn't matter how brightly they shine; only you know your true purpose, and you will find your key where it is, not necessarily where they are.

Your Purpose Is in Your Stories and Narratives

Even if you can't immediately identify your own purpose, you probably don't have to look very far. I do an exercise with clients where they draw out their career on a timeline with identified peaks of happiness and fulfillment and troughs of frustration or anger. They then talk it through, reliving what made them successful, passionate, and effective or what made them depressed, ineffective, or frustrated. Together, we identify the themes that have made them passionate. Even if that seems to be in anger. That anger about what you hate or what winds you up can help identify areas for your purpose. This exercise is fundamental to understanding how to shape your own path. The tears of joy or sadness that often come with the stories help identify the purpose.

And if there are tears, they often herald a positive breakthrough because the individual has begun to tap into what makes them passionate. Releasing that passion helps them understand how they want to live their life and lead others. More importantly, sometimes it points to how they don't want to live their life and lead others. What you don't want can be as important as what you do want in establishing a True North.

Establishing your purpose and its importance is vital to your journey of discovery. And leadership is the beginning of your story or narrative in taking your purpose and sailing it out of the harbor and into rougher seas. Sailing around the harbor with your purpose does not make for an engaging narrative or for progress. The dream of Martin Luther King Jr. could come true only when he launched it and engaged his followers to pursue great deeds and taking risks. In doing so, they created their own engaging stories of heroism that in turn engaged others. And so on, in a virtuous cycle.

You could do things the way they've always been done and wait for the point at which your work becomes average or in most cases irrelevant; or you could try something you've never done before. You could even argue that there's never a "right" thing to do, so you might as well embrace being wrong. But the worst thing you can do is not know why you're doing it. Your purpose, your True North, must be clear.

And in your stories is your purpose, and in your purpose is the energy that drives the team.

As I've already said, my purpose is "to create a measurable playground to disrupt the way people are led," and I constantly emphasize my personal mantra: "Outstanding only." It is a mantra that drives a "restlessly dissatisfied" mentality and shapes the way the purpose in the Pi2 model is attained. If you aim for outstanding you will get great. If you aim for great you will get good. If you aim for good you will get average. If you aim for average you will get poor. "Outstanding only" is the mindset for leaders.

Writing this book and going through multiple iterations and reviews has been driven by the belief that I need it to be perfect. Of course, that runs against the ethos of being more wrong and ignores the point that it can still serve my purpose. If I let go of the fact that not everyone will like this book, then I can put it out there, start a conversation, and then start my new, even better book...

And in doing so, I am practicing what I am preaching and modeling Pi2 as a system.

Practice What You Preach: Living My Purpose

I made the difficult decision to split from a business partner in 2007. The decision was based on a strong belief that to do what I do and what my team does, we needed to role-model. We had to practice what we preached. We were not doing this. And we were not pushing the boundaries of our role and industry.

The basis of trust is credibility. That credibility, and therefore whether somebody advocates for you, your business, your products, or simply whether to work with you, is based on you walking the talk. In my case, how could I teach or talk about leadership in being more wrong and Pi2 unless I walked the talk? It was not just a case of asking, "How might we practice what we preach?" That was not enough to fill the gap I felt we had. It needed to be, "How might we create a measurable playground to disrupt the way people are led?" Role-modeling how we might do that engendered trust and credibility in my role as leader.

We will be exposed to many sources of inspiration throughout our lives and careers. Some of us will, through encounters of suffering or hardship, derive a strength of purpose from that. Some will find themselves in, for them, unlikely leadership situations. Others will stumble into a situation that will cause a transformation in their lives. Others still will have a light bulb moment when out on a run. All will use their individual experiences to find their own path, forge their own purpose, or align themselves with like-minded others.

So What? Purpose

For each chapter in Parts Two to Four, I provide what one of my colleagues used to call the "So what?" In other words, "All the above synthesizes down into what?" The following are my suggestions of the system or systems and the habits I would apply to this area as a leader. They are examples—you should seek your own through experimentation.

Suggested System: Your Stories

The source of purpose, as explained above, is your stories. Just like I wish that my grandparents and my parents had captured their stories; I am starting with this book to capture mine. What are your stories that show your passion—love, hate, excitement, dread, fear? What can you crystallize from those stories that gets you jumping out of bed? What about those stories keeps you awake at night? Even better is to get somebody as a coach or buddy who helps you share stories and crystallize them.

Suggested Habits

1   Journal: Write a sentence a day about your actions and feelings
    (good and bad) from your life. Doing this as a habit each day and
    reviewing it with a peer or peers (see number 3, below) allows you
    and your team to keep your purpose at the forefront of your mind.
    Ask yourself: Is what I am doing today helping me be more wrong
    toward my purpose?

2   Write: Start writing letters to yourself or blog posts that help you
    shape your points of view, your stories, and your passions. It will help
    keep your purpose alive as well. Having to explain it to yourself—
    and, more importantly, to others—is the real test of whether or not
    it makes sense.

3   Do the deep work: Take a personal retreat every month to spend
    some time revisiting your purpose and your progress toward it. It
    does not need to be long. It can be with somebody as a sounding
    board or by yourself. My COO Sharon and I spend the end of each
    day on a call reviewing how the day went. We then plan retreats
    where we spend "deep work" time on what we are doing and what
    we are going to do.

4

identity

WE EACH HAVE an identity, whether we like it or not. Our
people, families, children—all have their views of us, consciously and subconsciously. And it matters. As a leader, no
matter how true and inspiring your purpose is, your identity—how
you are seen, what you are known for and identified with—is vital
to the success of your venture. It can attract and turn off followers
in equal measure.

For some parts of our identity, such as skin color, sexual ori-
entation, and birthplace, we have no choice. For others—such as
experimenter, polyglot, musician, cook, wine collector, storyteller,
cyclist, Republican, Democrat, climate change activist, climate
change denier—we do. This chapter is about choosing well in those
areas where we do have a choice. If we do not make our choices,
others will make them for us.

Remember, though: leadership is not a popularity contest. It
is not about choosing flexible identities that flow and change as
different people encounter you. It is about agitating for the future—
toward your purpose. You will have a view as leader about how you
want that purpose to be achieved. That is where the careful choice
of your identity and what you want to be known for will be a huge
influence on who follows you, how much passion they bring, and,
therefore, how successful you are.

What Is Identity?

In the Pi2 model, "identity" is "How you want to be known." It is how you want others to see you—and, more importantly, how they actually will see you. It is about how you make choices in how you handle challenges with face-to-face meetings, calls, setbacks, client feedback, and so much more. You cannot be everything to every-body; you need to decide what things are important to you and what quest you are on. Focusing on a few key identities and attributes and amplifying them allows followers to choose to follow you—or not—more easily. The focus also allows you to clearly measure the difference between how you want to be seen and the stark reality, or the pleasant surprise, of how you are actually perceived. Holding a mirror up to your identity allows you to develop or adapt how you bring yourself to your role.

Your identity is your brand. Outstanding brands, organizational or leadership, deliver on a promise. They generate an expectation—quality, leading-edge, different to market, fun, quirky, cool. They have a perceived value that takes them beyond comparison with similar products, goods, or services. They are utterly reliable and have a reputation that goes before them and makes them desirable. They also have an identity that others relate to—or not. They clearly articulate what they offer and allow the buyer or follower a clear choice to buy or not.

Choosing or Crafting the Identities That Work

Choosing the attributes you want to be known for is not easy. They can also change through time.

I am on my fifth iteration of my identity. When I first started crafting my identity, I was led by a list of what my colleague Robert Wylie would call noble statements that we would all hope to live up to. One of my first statements fell into that category: Honesty. I believed that's what I was and also wanted to be. I prided myself in telling the truth about what I thought. But when I road-tested the statements, I found out that having "honest" in your statement means that people expect you to live it every day in every moment. That would mean being honest about everything—other peoples' clothes, their look, their choice of lifestyle, whether I like them, rate them, or prefer somebody else to them. The feedback I got was that I was "selectively honest." That was fair. I tried to change it to "transparent," but it was not as meaningful. In the end, I went for "refreshingly direct." It has honesty at its core, but it is couched in being different and refreshing and exercising good judgment.

In our identity workshops for clients, honesty, reliability, curiosity, integrity, fairness, respect, and hard work are very popular as desired attributes. As Robert says, they are noble words that our heroes in stories have attached to them. If we have only a few words that we want people to remember us by, we want them to have impact. We work with leaders to build upon their choices of these words. Why do they want them? How do they define them?

For example, integrity has many different versions and translates differently in different cultures. Let's say you find a $20 bill on the street. What would you do with it? Some people's version of integrity would be about trying to find the owner. For some, it would be about giving it to charity. Some would choose to spend it not on themselves but on something for their child. Others would see integrity as fate and say that they found it, so it is theirs. Nobody is wrong. Integrity has different interpretations—what is yours? The fact that integrity was in the values of Enron did not stop them from being involved in a massive corporate scandal—one that also took down accounting firm Arthur Andersen. In the end, the choice needs to be clear and well defined so you can live and breathe it.

We must start choosing identities—and there will probably be more than one—that are true to ourselves, that we are able to live and breathe in all of our life, that are quirky and individual. Only when you bring your own little bit of crazy to the party does your leadership become true to you. The problem is that so many of us have had our bit of quirkiness squashed out of us over time, by parents and bosses, teachers and siblings. So we spend our time trying to rediscover that uniqueness and bring it to the fore.

Choosing and amplifying a quality in an identity statement also brings it under direct scrutiny from your team and all those who come into contact with it. For example, some would argue that honesty, integrity, and reliability are basic requirements for leadership, not differentiators. To differentiate yourself, you need something that feels unique, or at least authentic to you.

On a leadership level, the values you choose aren't just the values you'll stand and fall by—they're the values you expect your team and organization to live by. As a leader, you have to dig deep to find your core values or your deep inner drivers to establish your identity. If you are not digging at that level in yourself, it will show. They need to be those core values you would die for, or, in the case of aspirational identities, that you would contribute sweat, blood, and tears to deliver on. When we help leaders come up with their values, there is either a moment of brilliant clarity—"That's the one!" or "That's me!"—or a moment of what golfers call a "son-in-law" or "daughter-in-law": a shot that could be described as "not quite the one you wanted—but it will do!"

Interestingly, "I don't know what I want to be known for, but I know what I don't want to be known for!" is a helpful response in the choosing process. Much of the time, people find it easier to say what they don't want. Sometimes getting them to say, "I just don't want..." with a follow-up "Why?" will unlock some amazing insights. It's like choosing an "anywhere but here" direction for your journey: it tends to be a source of rich data. There's often good cause to reject something.

Once we have our identities, we need to test them in the real world. It is only by rigorously testing them in many different settings and with different people that we learn how much power they have—or how underwhelming they are.

The trouble all leaders struggle with is finding out how they measure up. The power gradient and the lack of trust means that having honest and open feedback about yourself is tough. One of my favorite exercises in leadership identity sessions is what we call "What Do You Think of Me?" As a facilitator, you stand up and ask the participants to go into pairs and write two lists—one of all the things they like about you and one of everything they don't like or don't trust about you. Give them permission to be as tough as they like.

In my experience, participants laugh and relish the exercise, getting into being direct and having a go at your shoes, your lack of belt, your hairstyle, and your attitude. "Too smooth!" "Too much like a salesman." "Too energized. You wear me out."

In the exercise, how you receive the feedback is also important. You don't want to be defensive. Ask, "What gives you that impression?" and "What makes you not trust me?" They are realizing that what you say and do has a big impact on perceptions. Once they have had their fun, it is then time to turn the tables and ask, "So, now, what do I think about you? You have made an impression on me too. I have three things I think about you. What do you think they are?" That's when they become uncomfortable. It is very hard for them to know what you think. But when you actually tell them and give examples of why, they are gobsmacked.

Part of the reason the whole exercise works as an opener is that it's jarring and gets people on their toes immediately. "What do you think of me?" is a strange question to ask because many of us are not used to being so direct with each other, especially when it gets personal. That's what makes this exercise so powerful. Your participants or followers are thinking, *There is this weird person giving me permission to say what I think about them with no risk.* It is also fun! *I'm being given permission in a formal business environment to be transparently honest with somebody.* Then there is the moment they realize the tables are turned, and that they have been giving off identity messages, whether they were conscious of them or not. But the great thing is, people do find it amazingly helpful to know what others think of them.

So, the lesson for your team is that as soon as we start interacting with other people, we form an impression of them, and they of us. This impression will be reinforced, modified, or discarded as we get to know the people better. But that first-impressions moment remains surprisingly powerful—not least because people never discuss it with each other.

The session does have its challengers: "I don't know you, so how can I tell you what I think about you?" Or, my favorite: "You are asking me to be something I am not. I don't care what people think of me!" Now, there is an identity statement. If you don't care what people think, great! Then you need to live with the consequences. Imagine a leader saying, "I don't care what people think!" What would be your view?

First impressions are incredibly useful for the person who receives them. It's rare that we know what people think of us. People resist giving this feedback because those thoughts, especially the first impressions, are strongly influenced by assumptions and preconceptions. We're taught to think of these as best kept under our hat, but an individual's frames of reference do have a remarkable power, and this power grows the longer the frames of reference go unchallenged. If we are aware of others' perceptions of us, we can do something about them—maintain them or change them. If we are not, then we are fighting in the dark to create a strong identity that is clear, coherent, and readily picked up by others. And they will still see you. You will be the one who doesn't know what they are seeing.

There is a CEO of a company in the United States who puts himself up for reelection to his role each year. He sees this as his check-in on how he is doing and whether he still has the license to lead. A core part of that will be feedback on how he is leading and the impact on his followers. It's a regular "What do you think of me?"

The audit on your leadership is useful for you to know what you need to change and adapt to get the most out of your team. It is useful for them to hear what you want to be known for first, so they can be specific with their feedback on how you are doing. Your identity, the how, needs to flex as a leader to the current reality. That feedback loop from your customers and followers allows you to change course or sustain your identity and how it lives through your habits and systems.

So What? Identity

Suggested System: Identity Experiments

Build a system based on conducting varying experiments around identities that work for you and your purpose. Play with words to craft statements. The first part is to identify the identity. For example, I was playing with the identity of being curious. I then felt I wanted to drive up the intimacy and risk in this, as per the Trust Equation introduced by David Maister and colleagues (we'll cover that in a couple of chapters from now), so I created "intensely curious" as an identity, giving myself license to dig deep quickly to understand others. I then tested it to see how it landed. For a year, I used it to create an impact in how I mastered coaching and my diagnosis work with clients. It then became something I was known for—and I moved on to a new identity experiment.

Suggested Habits

1   Use the power of three identities: Create three identities for yourself. Two should be strengths that you see in yourself and that others comment on; the third one should be a stretch for you, like my curiosity identity. Put them out into the world. Use them to talk about yourself and your work. When one of them does not work or has served its purpose, replace it with a new one that can be experimented with. Always keep to three. People struggle to remember more than three things you give them at once.

2   Create feedback loops: When you set out to test an identity, set up feedback loops with your biggest critics or people who will challenge you from another place. I use my clients to give me feedback by asking them, for example, to be "refreshingly direct" with me. One of my clients, Ian Holmes, thrives on that refreshingly direct feedback loop, knowing he can say anything to me and that I will act to change if it calls for that. Organize twice-yearly reviews with your people and clients that use your identity and its attributes as measures. Keep that feedback loop open as you develop your message.

5

presence

ET'S REMEMBER AGAIN the person or leader we found compelling: the one with confidence you inherently trust, conviction
in their identity, and that ability to connect with everyone
around them intimately. A leader at the top of their game. They are
wrapped in the almost indefinable cloak of presence. I say almost
indefinable not to spoil an illusion but to recognize and reinforce
that this compelling quality can be acquired, practiced, and polished, and that it can be worn as comfortably and authentically as
a second skin by anyone.

Presence comprises the perceived and real impact a leader has
on others, either through their in-the-moment interactions or via a
legacy built up over time. Your presence reflects your ability to be
agile in the moment and context. Presence is fluid and should be
seen as the appropriate dance to the music playing at the time. This
means understanding and developing your physicality and vocality. This will come only through deep, purposeful practice. Your
presence is made up of a series of habits and systems that provide
confidence in the people around you. Once you have mastery and
control over that, the art is in the ability to improvise in the moment
on a new dance floor, with different music and a partner you may
not have danced with before.

I have a secret to share. I wanted to be a dancer when I was a kid.
The ability to be fluid and move in time with music and changing

rhythms is transfixing when executed well. It is the same with presence. When someone like Maya Angelou, the civil rights activist and award-winning author, takes you on a journey of words, tone, volume, and passion, you are drawn in and engaged. For leaders, mastering this agility makes their changes in behavior seamless in the eyes of others.

But developing agility and mastery needs to be balanced with authenticity. We have all experienced that leader who has been on many training courses but comes across as entirely inauthentic. The levels of respect you earn and the mandate you create are based on the level of perceived authenticity you have with your team and in customer interactions. Even something as small as politicians using hand gestures taught at the school of "being a good politician" diminishes their impact.

That doesn't mean that smoothness is bad and roughness is good, however. When you are listening to someone with passion who keeps saying "like," "um," "ah," "basically," and has no coherent vocal punctuation, you struggle to hear past the noise to the message. When Jacqueline Farrington coached me, she would stand at the back of the room in my line of sight and every time I used a filler like "um" or "ah" or used my favorite expression, "Does that make sense?" she put her finger on the end of her nose. It seemed at one point she was in overdrive, her finger almost permanently on her nose. Surely, I was not making that many errors? But I was!

It is very difficult for us to hear ourselves when we are doing such things. The only sure way is to have someone capture us on video without us knowing we are being filmed. I once had that happen to me when I was a medical rep with Procter & Gamble. There I was, on camera in a playback of a training program, at the peak of my sales pitch on injections, captured clearly injecting an imaginary needle into my lifted buttock. Now, that was the moment I suddenly picked up on the need to increase my awareness of how my presence impacted others.

Authentic presence can be summed up simply as an accurate reflection in vocality and physicality of the true person you are.

However, this simple desire is aided or hindered by a complex, living human being: you. Your physical and mental health, how you act and sound, and how true it rings to your followers, what a nightmare of a day you have had, or whether you like or dislike the people in front of you—it all affects your presence and others' perceptions of your authenticity. People read it in you consciously or, in more cases than not, subconsciously. And then, as with their immediate first impressions of you, they are looking for more reasons to back up that judgment.

Presence = Gravitas + Prominence

In Pi2, presence is made up of two dimensions: gravitas and prominence. I first came across these terms when working with Jacqueline. Her background as a consultant and actress, and the fact that she is an excellent coach, allowed my clients and me to increase awareness about how to use these two dimensions. I thank her for that introduction and that work in progressing my leadership and the impact on what came next.

Gravitas

Imagine you have been working hard on delivering record sales with clients and getting rave reviews for what you have done, and you have been on your best behavior for a few days, and you arrive at your office. You head to the production area, where Della, the fun, cheeky woman who prepares all the boxes for the programs, is working with Linda, the head of the area. You pass a box of stress balls that you give as gifts to clients in workshops. You can't help yourself. You pick up a handful of those soft balls and before you know it, a stress ball fight has started around the office. People dive for cover. There's shrieking, cries of "Stop!" and "I'm on the phone with a client!" Ten minutes of glorious release as people end up laughing, trying to catch their breath, coming out from behind their desks. Then you get the feedback from your leaders: "Colin, that's your problem—you are too much of a lad! You lack gravitas!" How to pop a bubble of joy and energy. So what did they mean?

For many a decade, gravitas was the goal in organizations. The regular cry was, "They lack gravitas!" People—including me!—were sent off to work on developing that capability. But what was I looking for? It was an elusive property in my early career, according to my leaders. It was through my work with Jacqueline that I came to understand that gravitas is not the static, leaden quality my early leaders appeared to be looking for: it is best represented as a continuum. All along that continuum there are appropriate styles or behaviors that add value to particular situations.

The two ends of the continuum are high gravitas and low gravitas—like high gravity and low gravity. In her book *Gravitas*, Caroline Goyder describes high gravitas as "roots" that ground you and allow you to speak with weight and authority. Low gravitas is described as the "wings," with which an individual can provide levity and lighten the mood through humor.

We developed this further in Pi2: low gravitas gave us the Jester and high gravitas gave us the Interrogator. Both are real and symbolic figures from the courts of kings and queens. Historically, the jester's role was to brighten the monarch's mood. When things needed livening up and the mood needed to be lifted, the jester came out to perform by positively pumping light-hearted energy into the relationship—narrating stories of heroes, singing songs, and telling jokes—engaging and inspiring. When things were very serious, the jester sat at the side of the throne and subdued their own presence. Then the interrogators had their time. They asked serious questions to achieve rigorous clarity. They interrogated reality to ensure facts and accuracy for sound decision making. They became advisors on decisions that needed to be made—challengers and mentors.

Both Jester and Interrogator have an important part to play in the Pi2 model, and a leader needs to be able to live comfortably in both roles and agile in how they deploy the roles on the continuum.

As illustrated above, the positive impact of the Jester brings energy and lightness into the situation. It allows the followers and customers to feel energized and lighter in heart. The impact of the Interrogator is to bring clarity and alignment to the conversations and followers. The Interrogator works to assure everyone involved that they are on the right path.

Spending your life with your foot down on high gravitas would create a very serious environment and turn people away. Spending much of your time in levity and humor would drive people to wonder whether there was serious purpose to the leader. Agility and being able to flip deliberately and coherently from Interrogator to Jester is important. So, starting and enjoying a stress ball fight is great as long as it is balanced with serious work and achievements.

The fact that my leaders did not see my work with clients meant that they had only one view of my world. That was not their fault. It was my role to consciously manage the way I exerted my presence in all my relationships. Never forget who's noticing you.

Prominence

In Pi2, the dimension of prominence also has a continuum: how much or how little you are noticed.

Classically, we think of leaders as having a high profile. They lead from the front in suits and uniforms and with commanding words and action. They speak up in crowds, they make decisions, and they challenge others. A leader of that type has high prominence and is highly visible and noticed through their physical and vocal interactions. We call this character the Warrior: leading from the front with high visibility by doing, stepping forward, taking control, and always being in the thick of the action. There are many examples of leaders who have adopted Warrior mode—Greta Thunberg as she met one of her opponents, Donald Trump; Churchill when he delivered his "We will fight them on the beaches" speech; Gandhi at the front of a peaceful protest; Mandela guiding the Truth and Reconciliation Commission in South Africa after years of imprisonment and oppression. All are examples of front-foot leadership, high prominence, and shaping the direction of our future.

But there is also the leader who deliberately steps back to allow others to step forward. That is a fundamental pillar of leadership as well. Creating other leaders is a core purpose of leaders. To do that, leaders need to create space for others. We have labeled this role the Reflector. Let's be clear here: the leader never disconnects from the team or situation, even though they may be less immediately visible. They just consciously diminish their physical and vocal presence to allow others to feel they can step forward and own situations. The leader offers control to others. We have all been in meetings where the leader is sitting, listening, and positively engaged with the conversation, but has not spoken. The team and other leaders have the floor. The Reflector crafts a way forward for the team. And then one of two things happens: the meeting ends or the leader comes in with that powerful question that shapes a new or altered path. Both have power. The first is about trust and not fighting for voice share. The second is about course correction or acting as a guide.

Both leadership stances, Reflector and Warrior, have huge benefits. They also have clear differences in style and impact. The Reflector has the benefit of allowing followers to shine while they reflect and gather observations on the progress of the followers on the journey. The Reflector also has an impact on the individuals by encouraging their ownership and accountability. The Warrior has the benefit of kicking things into action and bringing life to strategy and purpose. Through their presence, the Warrior endows others with energy and purpose.

The Leadership Dance Floor

Together the dimensions of gravitas and prominence interact to create a leadership dance floor for us to play out our living the different styles and situations we face. In the Pi2 model, the Jester sits in the upper hemisphere with the Host and Energizer. This is because the Jester brings levity and lightness and adds energy to relationships and teams. In the lower hemisphere, with Disruptor and Catalyst, sits the Interrogator with rigorous clarity and alignment that brings a degree of risk to the relationship—challenging, guiding, disrupting, and catalyzing. Meanwhile, in the right-hand half with Energizer and Disruptor, the Warrior stands, generating action, stepping forward, and role-modeling through personal drive. And on the left-hand side with Catalyst and Host sits the Reflector, taking a back seat, observing, noting, and encouraging others to step forward and take ownership and accountability.

This dance floor provides a wide range of options that leaders can choose in their leadership behavior to adjust to different scenarios. The ability to dial up or dial down gravitas and prominence gives a leader options in dealing with any given situation. This is the lifeblood of a leader's agility. The key to it is brought to us in a rugby game analogy. In rugby, similar to football, a team seeks to carry and pass the ball to score a goal by breaking through the other team's defense and avoiding being tackled. We were always taught that when you tackle, "you need to tackle hard or you get hurt." Likewise, a leader needs to make conscious decisions in their approach and position they are in and "tackle hard." By doing that, they are demonstrating confidence and conviction. The fact that they can be agile and switch their style appropriately when the plan is first met with a change is about connection. Changing your position and approach quickly and as needed in real time is about being more wrong. Finding a way to be successful as a leader requires experimentation in presence.

As leaders, how we behave and interact with others needs to be finely judged and balanced. When my early leaders decided I "needed more gravitas," I was hurt: they had misread my decompression following client interactions; their view was of an immature operator. It didn't matter what I told them about how I was with clients. My goal was to be seen as a balanced leader, but I had not shown them the other side. I relied on them to teleport themselves into my client interactions to see what I saw. Dialing up and dialing down appropriately, as we shall see, is integral to each of the four leadership styles.

What I learned from that experience was that we have a choice to act in any way we feel fit to, but that action has consequences. Just as with choosing our personal identity, we need to be careful about how we choose to behave and about our impact on others. We leave behind us an "emotional wake," as Susan Scott describes it in *Fierce Conversations*. A leader leaves a legacy with that wake. The type of legacy is up to us to shape.

If those around you detect a false note, if you don't ring true, they will hold back from mandating you with their full trust. As a leader, your presence has to be authentic.

Business theorists agree that authenticity is an essential element of leadership. People know at a base level when someone is being dishonest. They want you to be straight with them. They might not like the message, but instinctively they want to place their trust in those who shoot straight. When I was a kid, I used to say, "Trust me! I'm a doctor's son!" It was meant as a joke, but I was playing on a fact: we trust people such as doctors, police, priests, and others in like positions. They are endowed with an authority that provokes an immediate sense of trust, at least until they break it.

Most leaders do not have that embedded trust a doctor or nurse has. They don't always have the important degree or qualifications. They rely on people trusting who they are and, as we have said, why they do the things they do. The key to building and sustaining that trust is the promise of authentic leadership. If your leadership style and approach is based on who you really are, then in theory it comes naturally. As I've said, my purpose is to create a measurable playground to disrupt the way people are led. Therefore, having a stress ball fight is as natural for me as being refreshingly direct.

As a leader, being authentic allows you to cast off facades or game faces you have used when under pressure. You can get on with putting your energy into leading, not trying to be somebody you are not, and into developing relationships based on mutual respect and understanding. If people are not attracted to your style or don't see value in it, that is OK. Avoiding wasting energy on trying to be something you are not is in itself a source of positive energy.

This is all easy to say, of course. But the fact is that most people have never deeply thought about what or who their authentic self is. They have given themselves labels or been given labels over time, of gender, class, personality, popularity, and so on. But those labels are at best like a zip code—that is, what general neighborhood you're in. What is your actual street address, so to speak—your authentic self?

It's worth defining what "authentic" means in this context. Simply put, purpose is the reason you do things, identity is how you want to be known in terms of your brand, and presence is the *you* you bring to the leadership role. Authenticity is about how true, reliable, trustworthy, or credible you appear in all areas, all the time. This is mainly measured by the consistency of how you show up. Since we're defined by what we do rather than what we say we're going to do, patterns of how you do things are an expression of who you are.

However, just as purpose can change, people change, so consistency as a measure is not the whole story. The process of learning through experience lasts a lifetime. Writing in the *Harvard Business Review* in 2015, Herminia Ibarra described what she called "the authenticity paradox." Too often, notions of authenticity are tied in with ideas of fixedness and singularity. But, Ibarra argues, "the notion of adhering to one 'true self' flies in the face of much research on how people evolve with experience, discovering facets of themselves they would never have unearthed through introspection alone."

What does Ibarra propose as the road to personal growth? Trying and failing and learning—in other words, being more wrong: "By viewing ourselves as works in progress and evolving our professional identities through trial and error, we can develop a personal style that feels right to us and suits our organizations' changing needs."

There is no doubt that the authentic self you bring to any task, if it is harnessed and challenged, will develop into a new authentic self. The learned behaviors, or more specifically habits, are the additional pieces that add to an evolving individual and leader.

Being authentic in leadership is about being agile and looking for opportunities to grow. It's about testing out behaviors and habits, seeing what you can grow into and retain as good while at the same time experimenting with what you can iterate around and change.

This is very clearly not about putting your game face on. It is not about seeking to conform. It's not about intimidating others with your air of immense distance, or hiding behind characteristics you think will protect you. It is about allowing you to experiment with habits and behaviors—keeping what fits and works and discarding what doesn't—while remaining authentic.

Within Pi2, authenticity must be linked to your values and core beliefs even if behaviors change. For example, I care deeply about inclusion and acceptance. As I learn more about that subject, my patterns of behavior will likely change, and as I practice new patterns, my behavior might sometimes be a bit "clunky." However, even if it is, it will be perceived as driven by my values and core beliefs of inclusion and acceptance, and so I am still being authentic.

Being authentic with your team is vital for building trust, connection, and engagement with them. There's also plenty of research to show that people work best when they bring their authentic selves to work. So if we are passionate about something in our lives, we need to bring it into our work. If we are passionate about honesty and speaking the truth, we need to live it at work or we subdue and betray ourselves. And if we are passionate about encouraging others to strive for perfection, we need to bring that to work. We know that leaders' behaviors set the tone for a team and an organization. Others find motivation in seeing someone who is the same at home, work, and through all situations, and who thrives being themselves. Finding the real you and an authentic pattern of behaviors is powerful. Mine are the patterns of disruption and playground, to which I add the spice of being refreshingly direct.

I remember doing an assessment for an associate and struggling to see how we could take him on. There was something missing. It was only through questioning that we jointly identified that he had, through training as an actor, suppressed his background and accent. He was told that he would be more successful if he did so. As an actor, he was very successful. However, he was wasting mental energy trying to be somebody he was not. That meant that he came across with less authentic power. I asked him to redo the assessment in his real accent and background. It was like night and day. He rocked it.

Similarly, in my early coaching days, I came across a coachee who had huge potential. He was a great manager, but for some reason he was holding back from also being the food-loving, gastro-experience-chasing person he was in his personal life. He always, no matter the heat, wore his jacket buttoned up. We probed away at the combination of the above and came to the stunning revelation that he was still, in his words, trying to live by his father's measurement system. The jacket was a symbol he struggled to lose. The impact on his work was that he could not bring his quirky, spice-loving side to his leadership. By making small changes and nudges, we started to get him to try and bring that to his work. He never abandoned the jacket, but he enjoyed the freedom he found in unbuttoning it.

Quite a few people I coach and work with are open about the fact that they are different people at work than at home. They admit that they almost switch personalities altogether as they walk through the office door. A large number of the people who read this book will have a similar view. As a coach and mentor, I see it as a life challenge to change that. To be somebody else takes effort, uses up valuable energy, and masks your true power. Authenticity is closely linked to reliability and trust because it allows others to know where they stand with you, and it means they know what to expect of you. In short, they get what they see and you are transparent to your very core.

And so we return to the importance of an individual's values as a leader.

Here's the rub: travelers launch themselves on voyages of discovery expecting to be transformed in some way by the things they learn, yet when it comes to the people we follow, we would like a level of consistency in how they act.

Yes, our purpose can change, but if we accept that our core values don't, then these are the foundations of our authentic leadership. When you describe authenticity in terms of what you stand for, it becomes easier to see how you can adopt a strong position through the process of change. It takes a lot of turbulence to skew a moral compass, though it's easy enough to forget to check it. Just ask all sides in the recent and current political debates in the United States and United Kingdom. Moral compasses are being shaken every day. Our values should be the basis of our True North. Our purpose might need to alter as we face different challenges and rougher seas.

And no matter how much you want your followers to be involved and invested, they still need to see your colors nailed to the mast. I had one of my critical moments as a leader in an exercise to define our organization's values. We were a day and a half into a two-day event. I had "played nicely with everybody" (read here: "sat on my hands, zipped my mouth, and squirmed") and had given everyone, in my view, a say. I was feeling good about taking a step back to allow others to speak. But it did not feel right—and later I found that it did not feel right for everyone in the room.

It was only when the facilitator pulled me aside that the light bulb went on. His feedback was simple: it was my team, my organization. People were following me and they expected direction from me on how the organization should behave. I had the right, and more importantly the responsibility, to state the values I held as true. My immediate, simplistic thought was, *Duh!* My deeper, more structured reflection was that here was one of the most common traps leaders fall into, particularly in large organizations: not being clear on your values and being afraid or reticent to bring those values to work and the team. Of the six values we had at the end of 2018 as a business, three were mine and the rest were the work of the team. Now, that feels like engagement. Values are the drivers of a lot of your presence as a leader and of the fact that people follow you, so it is important that you bring them to the party.

Caution: How You Act in Your Downtime Has a Big Impact!

Another key element of presence that is sometimes neglected is that the leader is not only the observer but also the object of observation by others—*all the time*. You have a personal identity whether you work on it or not. People are reading your identity, and you're making an impact as a leader, even in your downtime, when you are not consciously managing your behavior. Say an organization's leader becomes aggressive with a waiter over the food being late. All day, they have been professional; now that they're not at work, they let their hair down and out comes a flash of anger. And now you know something about them—as Dave Barry wrote: "If someone is nice to you but rude to the waiter, they are not a nice person."

These moments when you switch off and your real brand shows can be eye-opening in a positive way too—it's like that moment when you're at the pub with your coworkers and you witness a flash of humor and wit in a person who is typically serious at work.

So the next time you walk into the office in the morning, remember: if you are grumpy or angry, or if you are cheery and friendly, you set the tone for the office that day. As a leader, you are always on show—in your downtime and your uptime. But it is easier and less risky to be yourself than to constantly try to keep an act going. How conscious are you of the messages you are giving off? The microbehaviors that we demonstrate are the ones that our followers pick up on. The way we treat them impacts their treatment of others: we may drive them to copy our behaviors or, in many cases, avoid them.

How do we consciously set the right tone through our microbehaviors? By being conscious. How do we know the behaviors that upset our people and those that inspire them? By observing and asking. To truly understand yourself as a leader, you need to understand the warts-and-all impact of your behaviors on others.

It's about Respect, Not Being Liked

Many people seem to think that to be a leader, they need to be universally liked—that their presence somehow has to be liked, or at least likeable. My former manager taught me early that leadership is not about being liked. It's not a popularity contest. It is about respect. That is a key measurement of leadership. And to be respected, you need a consistent purpose, a clear view of what you stand for, what will you compromise on, and—just as importantly— what you won't compromise on. Being a professional irritant as a consultant or agitating for the future as a leader requires you to shake things up. Being liked is something you have to be willing to sacrifice for the sake of being an effective agitator. This means that when someone chooses not to be your friend or not to socialize with you outside work, it is not your failure as a leader. The real mark of a leader is that they respect your style and values and that you deliver for them. If they like you, that is a bonus.

So you can see that there are many different attributes and ingredients to presence. It never ceases to amaze me how rich the encounters are when I coach people on their presence. Rediscovering or determining your core values, bringing them to life through authentic patterns of behavior, and then applying rigorous practice to create a compelling, agile, and robust presence is incredibly rewarding. Bringing your complete and authentic presence to bear with clients and followers infuses all elements of the Pi2 model, as we shall see.

So What? Presence

Suggested System: The Mirror

The trouble with knowing how you are doing with presence is that you can't see or hear yourself as others do. Finding a way to create a "mirror" for ourselves as a system is important to keep us true to the impact we are creating. You can use technology, including videoing yourself or meetings. You can draw on trusted colleagues who are willing to be "touch your nose" guides for you, as Jacqueline Farrington was for me. You don't need to have ten hours of debriefing for every hour of "flying," as at the TOPGUN school. But the review is very important.

Suggested Habits

1 Use your colleagues as a mirror: Choose a colleague (or colleagues) who can be a mirror for you. Give them permission to call you on your behavior. It does not mean they need to touch their nose, but they can monitor and give you feedback. Who is going to be your "touch your nose" guide watching as you develop? Create a habit of debriefing with them.

2 Have a mindset warm-up: The neuroscience of presence tells us that the mindset we take into an encounter will impact the outcome. If I adopt the mindset of "hosting a dinner party with a glass of wine in my hand" when I run sessions, it drives me to relax and think about making connections and engaging the group. If I think of a mindset such as "my critics help me," I can go into feedback sessions with a curious, not defensive, attitude. Warming yourself up before meetings and events by crafting the right mindset is important.

3 Do a premortem on virtual presence: Doing a premortem before an event (working out what could go horribly wrong with an event) is a very useful technique. You can use it to think about everything that will impact your presence in the virtual world: distractions from your family or colleagues, the background in your screen image, audio notifications on Slack or Outlook, and broadband problems are all things that impact our presence. Sort out Zoom so that you are able to be properly, if virtually, present. Create a habit of predicting any issues and crafting solutions and contingencies so that meetings go smoothly and are effective for everyone.

THE THREE ENABLERS, purpose, identity, and presence, are all personal qualities that you can work on and improve. When we were designing the Pi2 model, we identified the fact that these have a disproportionate influence on a leader's impact—they move your performance or showing from good to outstanding. That translates into the confidence, conviction, and connection that people perceive and measure in their leaders. The manifestation of this all and the oil that lubricates the engine lies in the ability to lead one conversation at a time—tackling your toughest conversations first in a refreshingly direct way. Our next chapter sets out in detail what I mean by that.

Part Three

the conversation

6

refreshingly direct conversations

I MAGINE YOU HAVE been jailed for twenty-seven years and are finally released. The system that had oppressed you has been dismantled. You now have the chance to lead, and you can see the future as positive. How do you start?

Nelson Mandela began by having one conversation at a time.

It's a very simple philosophy in the best of times: you hold conversations of reconciliation with your oppressors, where all are free to air their views. Taking your time to hold those conversations with dignity, depth, and different lenses is a refreshing approach, especially when you have waited and suffered so long. For his reconciliation hearings in South Africa after apartheid, Mandela took the view that for his country to come to terms with what had happened and to move forward, it needed refreshingly direct conversations.

The Refreshingly Direct Mindset

When clients are asked to pick the most memorable expression of our business at Potential Squared International, the one that gets the most mentions is "refreshingly direct." They describe the experience of working with us as fun, engaging, and very challenging. But what really sets us apart is that we leave nothing unsaid in the room. We say the things that other people are thinking but are afraid to say. We also pick up on the unsaid in organizations and call it out. "Direct" is obvious from the fact that we are open with our views and thoughts. "Refreshing" comes from the fact that these are conversations our clients see as valuable. A bit like going for a sports massage, there are times when the conversations are uncomfortable. But they are a necessary part of leadership life, and the more you do them, just like sports massages, the less immediate your pain and the more effective you become in your performance and recovery.

As a leader, in order to be more wrong successfully, you need to develop a mindset that will clearly communicate to your followers a safe space for error, failure, and learning. The habits and systems you need to develop for this are embedded in the Pi2 model. The conversations you have within those habits and systems need to have that mindset as well. People need to feel that they can fail and make errors, admit them, talk about them purposefully, and learn from them. Remember: the great value of being more wrong comes in learning from it.

As L. David Marquet says in his book *Leadership Is Language*, the aim is to have bluework (thinking and planning) followed by redwork (action and experimenting) followed by subsequent periods of blue- and redwork. The conversations in the middle need to be rigorous in tone and to have an improvement or growth mindset to them. Embedding that "radical transparency" requires an awareness of the "power gradient," as Marquet calls it. The power gradient is never flat—leaders should have more power in decision making, but those decisions need to be made on the collective wisdom of their teams. Nurses should feel ready to speak their truth to surgeons. Flight attendants and copilots need to be able to speak their truth to the pilots.

Trust is the bedrock of leadership. In their work *The Trusted Advisor*, David Maister, Charles Green, and Robert Galford brought us the Trust Equation. In that, the elements of credibility (your track record) and reliability (delivering on your promises) are the basis for most good advisors and leaders. The real differentiators for trust, though, are intimacy (deep, at-pace building of understanding and therefore meaningful conversations and interactions that get quickly to valuable advice for the individual) and self-orientation (diminishing the self as the leader and advisor so the other person feels that it is about their issues). To build trust in the group of followers, the leader will need to deal with tough conversations. They will need to do that in a way that builds intimacy, such that their followers feel that they are deeply heard, deeply understood, and getting consistent value from being among the followers of the leader.

Conversations typically focus on what has already happened. As I mentioned earlier, when a TOPGUN pilot does flight training, they have up to ten hours of refreshingly direct conversations on just one hour of flying. The postmortem is rigorous and used to drive out insights and improvements to be made. But why wait until after? Why not focus on what will—or might—happen? And so there are now such things as premortems.

In *Harvard Business Review*, Gary Klein wrote of leaders who hold sessions during which they state up front that a just-planned project has spectacularly failed. They encourage the team to list every possible reason for failure, "especially the kinds of things they ordinarily wouldn't mention as potential problems, for fear of being impolitic." Klein gave the example of a session held at one Fortune 50-size company, where an executive suggested "that a billion-dollar environmental sustainability project had 'failed' because interest waned when the CEO retired." Another example of a reason for failure was "a dilution of the business case after a government agency revised its policies."

The leader then goes around the room asking each member of the team to read one reason from his or her list. This continues until all the different ideas are gathered from the team. After the session, the project manager reviews the list, looking for ways to strengthen the plan. This is a version of what I call "We are all doomed!" (See the BBC TV program *Dad's Army* for the reference.) Refreshingly direct conversations are a powerful way of stress-testing plans. In effect, it's moving forward by playing failure before you get to the real failure. It's a failure playground. And it can be a brutally effective one.

Another key point to be made here is that not every conversation needs to be a refreshingly direct one. The majority of conversations are social. Ordering your coffee. Asking how your day is going. Trying to help your daughter with homework. It is for the tough conversations and the ones that happen at critical points that you need to bring your refreshingly direct mindset. You also need to be ready to bring it when a social conversation turns into one of those critical moments.

I suggest that you deploy a technique that my former colleague Simon Scott used to use: "Stop, Pause, Reflect, Engage." It's a simple mantra to use at critical times. It also buys you time to make a judgment on the importance of having the conversation—rate it on a scale of 1 to 10. If it's 6 out of 10 or less in importance and is just about getting something off your chest, you reflect and choose to engage by not engaging. If it's above 6 out of 10, then you engage and tackle hard with a refreshingly direct approach.

The Refreshingly Direct Styles of Leadership

The conversations you have in all four styles of leadership need to have a baseline of being refreshingly direct.

As a Host, you actively establish networks of relationships and orchestrate the building of trust within these networks through encouraging, and facilitating, your team and customers to have refreshingly direct conversations. You will also have conversations like ones I have had many times about what it takes to thrive in your team and what is not acceptable in your team. Where necessary, you will have to let people go because they don't fit and your way does not work for them. And then you have to be prepared to be attacked by them and their people (in some cases their husbands and wives) for the "bad thing" you have done. As long as those conversations are conducted in the right spirit, it is the moment they realize that it was right to leave that provides energy to you.

Remember, though, realizing that the decision was right is not the same thing as liking the person who made the decision. At a leaving get-together for a client friend, a member of another of our teams stood up to say goodbye. During his speech, he recalled a conversation with me three years before. "At the time, I totally disagreed with Colin and did not like him," he said of me. "Three years on, I'm still not sure he is my favorite person, but in that conversation he was right, and I have been promoted twice since then on the advice he gave." It was a bittersweet moment. As a leader and coach, I was proud I had helped him. As a human, I was sad he did not like me. The words of my old boss Ian Ritchie echoed again in my head: "Leadership is not a popularity contest." Respect is what I held on to.

As an Energizer, you automatically generate a compelling story that has tensions and challenges that are going to require tough conversations. By choosing narratives that pitch growth and failing fast, you encourage your followers to look forward to robust and insightful conversations. They might not like them, but they will recognize they have value. Your team will learn to build their own resilience and ability to overcome barriers to success through that story and conversations with you.

As a Disruptor, you are starting to experiment and challenge. Challenging the human tendency to follow the path of least resistance requires refreshingly direct conversations. I remember doing an internal audit development academy for a major client. One of my team was running it. As the academy grew, new Potential Squared consultants needed to be added to the team. We had planned to start the week on the academy with a team get-together, including the client faculty, and briefing on Sunday evening. To avoid eating into their weekend, the established consultants decided on a shorter briefing and meeting immediately prior to kick-off on Monday. Looks like a small change, but in the eyes of our client, it had a significant negative effect on the performance of the new consultants—they were not ready and had not built rapport with the client faculty. The consultants were taking the path of least resistance, and the client director and leader, in this case me, needed to step in. A refreshingly direct conversation was needed to recalibrate and ensure we moved back to the successful playground we had created for our client's faculty and their participants.

As a Catalyst, you create a culture in which growth is actively promoted through both the sharing of insights and experience and the unlocking of personal potential. That "professional irritant" role of coach and mentor—the Catalyst—requires refreshingly direct conversations. Sometimes they can come in the form of repetition. Working with a senior leader in a fast-growing technology firm, I spent the three years of our relationship exploring a "being at school" reaction of proving himself to his senior leaders—he always waited for permission from them to take action. It was in the final three-hour coaching session, about ninety minutes in, when the light bulb moment came. Before that, my role in a refreshingly direct way was to hold the mirror up to him. At the ninety-minute mark, he said, "I got it!" It was a bit like in the film *Forrest Gump* where he has been running for years and then suddenly stops. We looked at each other, and I said, "What do you want to talk about now?" The answer was the most amazing one for me as a coach: "Nothing. I get it now!"

Refreshingly direct, especially in coaching or mentoring, can take time to have positive effect—even three years. That infinite mindset is about creating the habits and systems that sustain the individual's performance. I coach that person even now. But we don't need to cover the "school" reaction anymore because it now is self-corrected.

Let me be clear from the outset about two things: first, as mentioned before, not all conversations need to be refreshingly direct—ordering a coffee or asking someone to do something that is part of their role does not require being refreshingly direct; second, being human means that we would also like to have a filter on the amount of feedback we receive and when we receive it.

I used to say that I loved feedback. It was only when one of my colleagues pointed out that sure, I loved hearing it, but I did nothing about a lot of it that I realized that changing as a result of the feedback is even more important than being open to it. For many people, focusing on one or two things to change, like habits, is all they can handle at one time. Therefore, refreshingly direct conversations need to be part of a system of learning and, as such, to be appropriate and timely.

The grounds for these conversations will be all too familiar to you: at work, at home, or with clients. Usually something is wrong, or at the very least not right, and whether it has been expressed yet or not, it is "known." It is probably festering away, eating energy and being built up in someone's mind as difficult or tough to such an extent that they avoid the conversation, or at least avoid telling their own truth—or, even more importantly, seeking the other person's truth.

Being more wrong is immensely helpful here. We know that to learn from successes and failures, we need the ability to rigorously interrogate the facts and lessons. In the Pi2 context, when the wider team is aligned to a common purpose, in some ways it makes the conversations easier. There is a mutual goal to help guide the outputs. We can then be more objective about the failure, as it is in the common good. If we set the failure up to be a good thing, as it is about learning, then it becomes even easier. The fact is, though, that failing and admitting it is not easy. The common purpose makes the conversation refreshing; the search for learning encourages the directness.

Having and purposefully practicing refreshingly direct conversations with your team provides you with experience and a rough template for involving your clients in your "fail early, fail often, fail forward" journey when difficult conversations with them are necessary. It is also about having those conversations with yourself. Difficult conversations are the most valuable. These are what author

and leadership guru Susan Scott refers to as "fierce conversations"—
the ones in which you get to what's really going on, when people let
down their defenses and share insights that can be very valuable.

The Leadership Language

I have mentioned L. David Marquet's book *Leadership Is Language*.
He makes the obvious but often overlooked point that leaders need
to work on the language that enables their teams to feel "psychologically safe" to fail and learn fast. The book uses the story of a
cargo ship that sinks in a hurricane in the West Indies. All of the
crew members die, but the voice recording of the bridge maps out
how the language of the captain and crew caused fateful decisions
and lack of decisions to save themselves. The captain laid an egg of
doubt early in the journey by saying that only weak people change
course. That egg of doubt hatched into decisions made by the rest
of the crew while the captain slept. For leaders and teams who are
sailing their ship in rough waters, the language of learning and collaboration is needed, not the language of disapproval and fear.

We can take this further if we link it to your confidence, conviction, and connection and demonstrate how it directly impacts on
your ability to be refreshingly direct.

Confidence is about the ability to balance the dimensions of
presence. To step back to allow space for the team to step forward or
to step back in to guide the ship. The language is subtle in its change
but powerful in its impact. And in this case the captain closed the
door for his crew to invite him back in. Look at the difference in
impact between a question such as "What's on your mind?" versus
"What have you got to report?" Consider the difference between
"What do you like about the idea? What do you wish for the idea?
What do you wonder about the idea?" and "What do you like? What
do you not like?" It's all in the language (and silence) the leader
uses. It's in asking a powerful question such as "What's the real
issue?" and then leaving silence to do the heavy listening, as Susan
Scott talks about in *Fierce Conversations*.

Consider the disparaging language used by the captain that clearly expresses his conviction that only weak people change course. In seeking to disprove the captain's conviction that they are "weak," the crew don't change course and so lose their lives. As Marquet writes, my language should be about "improve," not "prove."

And it cannot be said that the captain's language demonstrated any connection with his crew. This is where the language of empathy, emotion, and culture is brought into the mix. The ability to show curiosity for the feelings and thoughts of others and to act in accordance with those ideas is at the core of being empathic.

Just imagine how different the outcome would have been if the captain's approach had involved a purposeful, refreshingly direct conversation.

The Conversation Ingredients

To have refreshingly direct conversations effectively, you need to deploy a refreshingly direct mindset. Most people focus on the "direct" bit. It is the easiest to comply with—say what you think and mean at all times. "Refreshingly" is the more difficult on which to focus and execute. "Refreshed" is the overall feeling someone has when they come away from being dealt with in this way. And what does that refreshed feeling stem from? The simple answer is that the person feels energized, motivated, or liberated. So many of the conversations my team and I lead with a refreshingly direct mindset are validated by a claim from the other party that they have never had such an open and energized conversation. "Nobody has been that honest with me before," they say. "I never have felt able to have such an honest conversation"; "It seems that you are really listening to me."

Part of "refreshingly direct" lies in a mindset that Scott raises in *Fierce Conversations*: we go into difficult conversations holding 50 percent of the truth and our goal is to seek the 50 percent of the truth the other person holds. Building on this, a refreshingly direct mindset is about telling and discovering truth. The telling is intuitive in thought and feeling—the ability to call something as you see it. The discovering is engaging in an open and curious debate with the other person or people and finding their truth. Part of being refreshingly direct is being aware that many times, you are just acting as a Catalyst and the solutions or actions are created by the other person you have "agitated" through telling and seeking. The playground for the refreshingly direct mindset is the conversation.

Like all purposeful conversations, refreshingly direct conversations have a basic framework:

1   a simple opening and follow-up,
2   being intensely curious,
3   listening and providing time for someone to feel listened to,
4   giving advice or jointly finding a solution, and
5   agreeing on outputs and linking back to purpose.

Let's now look at important aspects of some of these steps.

A Simple Opening

The opening to any conversation is massively important to its output. The consistency of the opening in conversations can create a real sea change in the culture of a team. In *The Coaching Habit*, Michael Bungay Stanier uses two types of questions that resonate with me. "What's on your mind?" is a beauty of a question. In the hero's journey, it reinforces the leader's role as guide. The content of the conversation has shifted to the coachee or follower. They own this conversation. The Catalyst or coach is just there to be a professional irritant. The next question from Michael's list, "And What Else?" (or "the AWE question"), encourages the sense that the leader has all the time in the world. Most people don't have the time and destroy the integrity of the relationship by diving straight into solutions or the issue.

Being Intensely Curious

Being "intensely curious" is a value of our business that I deployed from one of my identity experiments mentioned earlier. It is a value that bridges all elements of the refreshingly direct conversation. Curiosity is the defining trait of the innovating mind and therefore of the Disruptor. Curiosity is also the trait underpinning both mentoring and coaching—the Catalyst. All too often, the truth is that leaders don't find the time for curiosity, let alone coaching or mentoring. This can be reinforced by the sense that when things are going well, you don't need coaching, and when they're going badly, it's not a priority. I'd argue that coaching is vital all of the time, and it doesn't have to be a great burden. I suggest that you make being a Catalyst a habit and keep that to regular short periods of time. Coaching can be done in a series of five-minute conversations. And it's better than an annual review: it means that you know what's going on all the time and can pick up on opportunities to learn and immediately address problems and concerns.

The concept of being "curious not furious" strongly appeals to me. It suggests that the points of connection are not just the bubbles that rise to the surface—they are also there for you to search out. In the "experiment" and particularly the "challenge" areas of the Pi2 model (under Disruptor), this requires us to be truly listening and curious. As Stephen Covey wrote in *The 7 Habits of Highly Effective People*, seek first to understand before being understood. This is backed up by Susan Scott's principle of holding only 50 percent of the truth.

Listening and the Power of Being Listened To

A number of times, my team or I have had the feedback that we are telepathic. We have the ability to pick out what somebody is thinking or feeling from seemingly nowhere. What's our secret? It is all to do with the three levels of listening. The model is a pillar of our work in all aspects of personal effectiveness.

Level 1 listening is the base level of "waiting for the chance to speak." Everyone does this. We are listening or pretending to listen to the other part of a conversation but our mind is elsewhere, remembering stories that need to be told, selecting arguments or facts that back up our position, waiting for the pause from the other speaking parties so we can get our views in play. We are doing our best to look as though we are listening. Nodding like all good leaders do. Saying, "Uh-huh" and "Great" with the best of them. But the truth is that we are doing very little true listening.

Level 2 listening is called "active listening." This is all of the good things we have been taught to do when listening: summarize our understanding, make eye contact, ask probing questions, take notes, restate points, dial back to what was said earlier, all while sitting at a ninety-degree angle and turning our heads to show we're listening. The act of purposeful practice is alive and well in mastering these skills of Level 2: paying real attention to what the person is saying.

So, then, what is Level 3 listening? It is paying real attention to what the person is not saying. What are the unspoken messages from the person in front of you? *Captivate* author Vanessa Van Edwards uses her obsession with the TV show *The Bachelorette* to highlight the ability to pick up on what the gambling community calls the "shows" or "tells" in people's body language that give you a true story of what is going on. In her example, the voice of the woman on the program is saying yes to her prospective partner, but her body language is screaming no. Van Edwards offers a list of programs to watch with notes on body language and microbehaviors that allow listeners to read their conversation partners. This is the way to be seen as telepathic.

Being a leader and coach, my experience is that the simple act of listening to someone or being listened to releases a huge amount of stress and anxiety. The Headspace app and meditation have taught me that the traumas and issues of our life can be described using the analogy of standing in the middle of a busy road with cars coming at us from all directions. In life, we are often confused and stressed, not knowing what thought or feeling to tackle next. Meditation teaches you that this is normal and that you need to find a way of mentally stepping off the road, still allowing the thoughts to come but choosing the ones to deal with. The only thing is that, as a colleague once told me, "we cannot tickle ourselves": there are some things for which you need another person. Team members storing up anxiety and stress are a core part of what leaders deal with. Having someone to listen to you—a coach, mentor, or combination of both (Catalyst)—is an essential part of dealing with life. That listener, being a sounding board, is another role of a leader through conversations—refreshingly direct or the garden variety.

I consistently get the feedback that, because I appear confident and do what I do, people are surprised that I continue to need coaching and mentoring. However, the lifelong learner mindset is essential to strong leadership. That includes the chance to be listened to and have our ideas and insights shaped. I sit each year in an annual business retreat for an organization called ISA. It is a gathering of the top learning and development organizations in the world. We listen to renowned keynote speakers such as Margaret Heffernan and Patrick Lencioni. We share the challenges we face as organizations and seek our peers' and competitors' help in finding answers to our problems. The annual retreat has generated a space for us to be listened to. The comfort that comes from realizing that we all share the same problems never ceases to amaze me. As lifelong learners, we learn on both sides of any conversation as long as we have the right mindset.

There is no more obvious giveaway that someone has been through a Design Thinking process than when they structure their feedback using the "I like, I wish, I wonder" format. The feedback sandwich of the past has gone. The positives and negatives have been replaced with language that has a growth mindset embedded in it. "I like that this book has stories in it, Colin." "I wish you had written it sooner." "I wonder whether the lack of research to the model might turn some people off." Now, that is feedback I can deal with; it gets me thinking about how I might address the "wonder"—if I need to at all. The "like" is a starting point for what is going well and is positive about an idea. The "wish" points to areas of possible improvement. The "wonder" brings a refreshing nature to the feedback in that it is a conversation starter, not a fait accompli. It offers a suggestion and prompts thought for questions that remain to be answered and ideas that are still to be had. It might be brave to raise, but it is done in the spirit of exploration and growth. In the same spirit, the path has been cleared for giving advice, where appropriate, and jointly finding a solution.

Clear Outputs of Conversations and the Link to Purpose

All refreshingly direct conversations should have a set of outputs linked to the overarching purpose. What that means in simple terms is asking yourself why you feel the need as a leader to have the conversation. As mentioned above, use Simon Scott's "Stop, Pause, Reflect, Engage" approach to deal with any tough spot or decision making point. The Reflect stage offers the simple question, "How much is this conversation worth to you on a scale of 1 to 10—10 being incredibly important?" We often launch into conversations without being clear on why, particularly in the heat of the moment; if we ask ourselves this question, we can give ourselves time to reflect on the real reason we are about to open our mouths. As I mentioned earlier, it's amazing how often we dive into a conversation just to get something off our chest. When we realize this, we see that the impact of that conversation might be in the short term to feel temporarily relieved, but the risk is the longer-term damage that it does to our relationship with the person in front of us. But if the value is above 6 out of 10, then the conversation is needed. We are also now clearer on why and on the outputs required from both parties. Refreshingly direct conversations provide you, your clients, and your followers with outputs that drive toward a core purpose.

It's a wonderfully refreshing concept and pays dividends in the smooth and tight running of your ship. Like everything else, it benefits from purposeful practice, and it needs to be employed appropriately and at the right time. As we look at the four styles of leadership in Pi2, we will discover how that might be done.

So What? Refreshingly Direct Conversations

Suggested System: Team Bucket Dumps

My team and I have what we call "bucket dumps" at the beginning of meetings. There is no agenda—it's just a chance for everyone to whine, if they want to, about everything in their work life—or their personal life, if that works better. It started as a formal process but has now moved to a Daily Pulse call. We use this habit to allow people to feel they can say with candor when they are having a good or bad day. Once it is in place as a system, it becomes OK to truthfully reveal how you feel.

Suggested Habits

1   Pay it forward: Start tough conversations with a mindset of paying it forward. If you have determined that the conversation is worth more than 6 out of 10 for you and the person, go in asking yourself, What can I do for that person?

2   Be intensely curious: The habit of holding the mindset that "knowledge speaks, wisdom listens" (as Jimi Hendrix is often credited with saying) leads you to be curious going into refreshingly direct conversations. Make the other person feel listened to.

3   Create a third island: Difficult conversations sometimes feel as if you and the other person are on two different islands. In group conversations, there can be multiple islands. You have your position (your island), they have theirs, and it can become a case of defending your island and lobbing stones at the other people's islands. The idea was created in a coaching session with a CEO who would invite his team

to his island for them to be convinced of his points. Of course, they complied with his view, but he was trying to get them to share theirs. He would use a whiteboard to draw and shape the conversation by mapping their agreements and challenges. The whiteboard became the third island: a joint island that was neutral territory and acceptable to both.

the four leadership styles

7

host

REGARDLESS OF YOUR preferred style of leadership, you need to be able to build rapport and make your connections and followers feel special. I call the highest level of this "The Kirsty Role," after my sister, Kirsty Clarke. We run Academies for Internal Audit Professionals for our clients, and Kirsty's role is to ensure that everybody is in the right place at the right time and feels welcomed. She takes that role to another level: she has the ability to make people feel special through simple but powerful actions. And if Kirsty invites you to dinner, it is never just dinner—it is a moment when you are invited to tell your story, pour your heart out, and be entertained by your own stories. She provides an audience and invites others to share in that experience. She is curious and helps others feel special. But it is even more than that. Kirsty's ability, through observational curiosity and listening, to pick up when something is wrong or what is being left unsaid is uncanny.

Some people have an amazing array of interpersonal abilities. They seem to have an ability to attract to them the widest range of people from different backgrounds, thinking styles, opinions, and passions. They then have this other unique ability to bring the right combination of people together for varying reasons, like project groups, in new companies, for dinner parties or just social occasions. Once they have those people together, they seem to have an inbuilt sense of how to bridge the gaps of authority, culture, language, beliefs, and styles. They are comfortable gently agitating conversations, guiding different groups of people to do things they would normally not do, and facilitating a safe place to air views and share opinions in the spirit of deep and powerful conversations. They seem to know when to step in, step out, observe, comment, and even lighten the mood.

Such people are consummate Hosts, embodying everything necessary to connect and engage with the different worlds they inhabit. This chapter is about them, and it has two parts, the first for the Host as they connect and the second for the Host as they engage.

Host: Connect

I'm taken back to being twenty-one years old and sitting on a porch in a rocking chair, in Montreat, North Carolina, in the Blue Ridge Mountains. I am talking with Randy Taylor and am captivated as he smokes his pipe and talks about his life and the current political situation.

Randy has the ability, in his fifties, to make me feel, as a twenty-one-year-old with a small percentage of his experience and wisdom, as if I am a special person worth listening to. He is a minister—at that time, he was also the head of the San Francisco Theological Seminary. He had been a student of my grandfather's and talked with reverence about how my grandfather used to conduct his deep conversations and tutorials while fishing the salmon rivers of North East Scotland. My grandparents had taken Randy and his wife, Arline, in as guests when Arline was expecting their first child, Katherine. The families had been close ever since. In 1972, at the age of seven, I had the then-unconscious privilege of meeting the parents of Martin Luther King Jr. at dinner in the Taylors' house in Atlanta. In the late 1950s, Randy had promoted a relationship with the mostly black Church of the Redeemer in Washington and its pastor, Rev. Jefferson P. Rogers, at a time when such arrangements were unusual. When the leadership of the Southern Presbyterian church declined to officially support the 1963 March on Washington, Randy turned the Church of the Pilgrims into a base for its members who attended, and he led the group to the march. He also participated in civil rights marches in Selma, Alabama, in 1965. It was on a flight home from Selma that he and other ministers helped conceive For Love of Children, a group formed initially to help abandoned and abused children housed in Southwest Washington's overcrowded "Junior Village." Now, as he sat there talking to me, I basked in the man he was.

Randy had the ability to listen and engage as a leader. He had brought three million Presbyterians together in the reunion of the South and North churches in the United States. He had to tackle years of differences. As an article in the *Washington Post* outlined after his death, "As a representative of the Southern branch, he worked to prod its leaders toward accepting the long-standing overtures of their Northern counterparts, in the process brooking cultural and political differences over race, rites and the role of women."

Randy had that unique ability many of us strive to achieve, to bring even his strongest critics and enemies into a circle where dialogue and progress could be made. As leader, you need to attract followers to your True North by crafting and living a compelling story. You want followers to connect with your purpose, and therefore you need to be living a life that promotes that authentically. Randy did that and made me, and everybody he met, feel special at the same time. But he was never the center of attention. He stepped back to allow others to shine. He hosted conversations and gatherings to allow others to share their truth and wisdom. He was never afraid of tackling a tough issue. He made it feel reasonable that solutions could arise for the toughest of problems.

The skills of the Host are about creating systems and habits that provide an inviting space for people to connect with others who share a passion and purpose. Here, people can share their truth, amplify their voice, feel part of a team, and start to shape their own and the team's future. I was lucky to meet Randy and considered him an adopted father. I sometimes took it for granted—until I tried to recreate his abilities as a leader. Then I realized how the systems and habits Randy had created were based on hard work and a genuine desire to lead.

I was lucky a second time when I started working for Ian Ritchie at The Oxford Group. He had that same ability to relate to me, inspire me, and surround himself with difference. I felt at home—it was a place where I could take risks and shine. I was trusted, treated like an adult, and allowed to shape my own leadership skills—with successes and a large amount of being wrong. Ian gave me space, and a huge opportunity to move to Paris and head up the international business. He gave me rope and I always knew that if I failed, he was there to support me. Even when he chose one of my colleagues over me for a senior role in the business, he did it in such a way that I learned from it. My pride was dented, but I knew exactly what I had not done and what I needed to do.

Ian never lost my engagement or my connection. When he led us in the challenge to resurrect the business from a significant downturn and a series of redundancies, he gathered us around a table—the group of people was a real mix of opinions and backgrounds. He gave us all a classical music CD with an inspiring focus on rebirth and regeneration. His work with us all and the wider team connected and engaged us to transform the business back to its former glory.

So how did Ian and Randy do this?

Pay It Forward: A Relationship Is Not Just for When You Need It

The role of the Host is complex yet simple. The main rule of being a Host is that, just as "a puppy is not just for Christmas," so network building and relationship management is not just when you need it for job hunting (when you lose your job) or recruitment (when you lose your team members). The cultivation of "relationships with a purpose" is a full-time role. Connections that you make one year can bear fruit three to five years along the line. Relationships that you neglect and don't nurture fade away and become less and less promoters and more and more neutral or detractors.

Every day of our lives we are faced with moments that define how relationships develop or fail. The conversation with a candidate when you reject them for a role can be the reason that they, having been treated in the right way, still recommend you to a friend. That is how I got the job at The Oxford Group—through my friendship with Haydn Rees, one of the other people in my MBA at Durham University. He went for an assessment and failed—but in the debrief, he recommended me and one other person. The rest is history. The fact that many years later Haydn became a member of our team was part of that relationship journey.

The fact is that most successful networking is about the principle behind the expression "pay it forward." How do you sustain a system of relationships or connections, in your team, the industry, with your friends, and in your network, that provide you with a source of minds and actions that can come together to create change and energy for your quest as a leader? Not by simple quid pro quo. Sow seeds, fertilize, cultivate, build a "human ecosystem."

Building that "human ecosystem" is an intrinsic part of any person being successful, whether they call themselves a leader or not. It is a way of making connections to engage people in what you stand for and in your direction of travel. It is about stretching your reach to people who might challenge your thinking, disrupt your way of operating, and take you to the next level. It is a system that thrives on difference and, as Nassim Nicholas Taleb says, is not just resilient but antifragile—it thrives in the roughest of seas and the greatest of challenges.

However, achieving this level of antifragility requires constant and careful nourishment, just like a good personal training program. It takes rigor to be on top of the habits in the system. You work the connection points for your network, you turn up for people before they need you, you start on the front foot with paying it forward. You build a "bank account" for the relationships that allows you to ask for things in return, and when you pay it forward to some-one, you focus them to in turn pay it forward to others.

What you give to your network is so much more important than what you may take. We have all been "networked" negatively at some point and we all know someone we'd prefer to avoid at any networking opportunity. In his book *Give and Take*, Adam Grant makes the link between individual success and having a mentality of giving; I use the term "pay it forward," from the film of the same name. In case you haven't seen the film, its premise is this: The hero conducts an experiment wherein he does something good for three people without expecting anything in return apart from that they pay it forward to three other people. One of the people he helps is a homeless character, and the protagonist thinks he has failed in helping because he sees no immediate return on that favor for others—the homeless man seems to just disappear. However, suc-cess comes in many unseen ways, and the homeless person later saves a woman's life as she tries to jump from a bridge. The film culminates in a demonstration of the exponential impact of one individual who has been kind in turn. The human ecosystem has delivered through the influence and impact of one individual.

The opposite is true as well. I have a connection who has been a friend and colleague for many years. I have, in the spirit of pay-ing it forward, helped them in many cases—and still will. But they have not paid it back or, to my knowledge, paid it forward to others in the same way. At one point, I introduced them as an option for a client and subsequently found that they had gone ahead with a piece of work without letting me know. The client should have had more integrity, but I expected more from the connection. Would it stop me from helping them again? No. But I feel on the cusp of a "refreshingly direct" moment. My hope and belief is that my approach will pay dividends for someone in their network. That is a mindset that must be held to keep the spirit of connection alive.

In networking terms, what are the benefits of paying it forward when attracting your followers? One benefit is in how you are per-ceived as a networker. When you head into a networking event or a meeting with a person with the goal of helping others rather than focused on what you can get from them, you become in their eyes someone who can help them rather than someone to be avoided. And people relax and become more open in an environment where there are no strings attached. You are creating a rapport that will make any future contact easier, and you are comfortably networking without an agenda. You find yourself in a position of strength by not expecting anything in return.

People with a short-term view tend to avoid paying it forward. It is true that when you try this approach you are leaving yourself vulnerable and open to exploitation. You are certainly giving yourself more opportunity to be wrong. But, as Grant concludes in *Give and Take*, the giver will reap the rewards for their approach.

As a business, we at Potential Squared have practiced the "pay it forward" mandate for many years and have seen great success with it. We have helped relationships. People's sons and daughters have gained work experience or made valuable connections. We have exchanged free coaching. There is no immediate return, and sometimes the return comes from contacts of contacts who have heard the story. It is perhaps a fact that we, as humans, will naturally focus on the relationships that don't work. However, that shouldn't make us discount the hundreds of successful relationships that pay dividends for others as well as ourselves from the simple act of paying it forward.

However, experience has taught me that unless paying it forward is combined with a direction we are going in, it can be too speculative an approach and can leave us spread too thin and with no clear strategy. I have found paying it forward is most successful when combined with my philosophy of "relationships with a purpose."

Relationships with a Purpose

So your network is vibrant and antifragile. You have a source of capable people from different backgrounds and with different skills, attitudes, and cultural backgrounds. As a leader, your role is to craft the right mix of personalities, capabilities, and potential for an unstoppable team. So how do you bring them together? The start of the process, before you are in engage mode, is to have a clear relationship with a purpose for your connections. That can be in the internal team you lead and also in the client group you select to work with.

When I teach this approach in a workshop, it gets a mixed reception. The simple premise is that every relationship in your life has a purpose. The nature of the context and our background drives how the relationship should develop. That starts with the relationship expectation: the salesperson in the car showroom, the mother to the daughter, the teacher to the pupil, the leader to the follower. It continues from there.

My relationship with my daughters, for example, carries the expectation that I act as a father for them for the rest of their lives or mine. Why I do that is also important. In theory, that purpose and its expectations have been defined for me by others—by our culture and family. But are they really? My view is that I might have the same zip code of the "parent" identity as many of my friends who are parents, but they don't live at the same house as me. It is for me to shape my purpose for the relationship with my daughters. And the purpose might be different for each of them. The common element for both is that I provide a space for them in which to grow, love, and learn. I do this through creating a playground for them to experiment in. The force of my influence in that relationship is important. Too light a touch and they don't feel I care or am engaged. Too heavy a touch and they don't have the space to learn. The first thing I do, though, is have in my mind the sense of direction and the freedom to act that I want for them.

My relationships with my clients are, in many cases, much the same in their purpose and expectations. I need to make a judgment on how much of a sense of direction I provide and how much freedom I give them to act. The power base is also a similar issue here. In theory, I have the power in my relationship with my daughters; with my clients, in theory, it is the other way around: they have the choice to work with us or not. But to be an effective father to my daughters and partner to my clients, the basics are the same: I need to be trusted. I need to have a track record and approach they both trust and respect. I must have the ability to foster the right degree of closeness, understanding, and "intimacy," as David Maister and colleagues say in *The Trusted Advisor*. I also must make them trust that my focus is on them and the benefit I can provide to them. And that means I must have a clear sense of my purpose in that relationship.

For a lot of people, the clinical nature of analyzing a relationship and its purpose may feel cold and calculating. But unless we analyze and focus on it, we are putting our trust in luck. There is a strong possibility that we do something successful for us and, by chance, important for them—but why would you want to trust in luck? As a leader, purposeful practice in building and nurturing a human ecosystem that is fundamental to your success requires you to have a purpose for each of the crucial relationships in that system.

Choosing Your Relationships

The challenge that many of you will have in your heads at the moment is, *How do I manage the volume of the relationships I have as a leader?* I'm sure you are thinking, *That's a job in itself without even starting to do what you are asking me to do!* For a leader, the feeling of being overwhelmed by relationships is a real problem. I coach a lot of people in many different organizations who are working in the "driven achiever" space that Jamie Smart describes in his book *Clarity*. We are trying to be everything to everybody with the delusion that that is what it takes, and that is what the receiver of that "diluted experience" is asking for. We need to be "properly selfish" and almost ruthless in how we choose to spend our energy with our relationships. So how do we do that?

It comes back to purpose—and a clearly defined map of your relationships, their purposes, and their relationships to each other. When you have defined your relationship map and categorized the areas in which you are lacking that you want to beef up for better impact—or, your "buckets" you need to fill—then you can start to prioritize. We can choose the technical skills we need and recruit

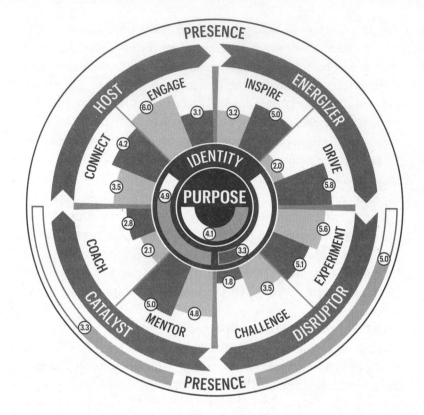

for those (sales, customer service, innovation, leadership, finance, marketing, internal audit, and many more). We can choose the cultural and attitudinal characteristics that we want and recruit with attention to that. I love the ones that ExperiencePoint, one of our partners, look for: "humble, hungry, smart"—simple with clear definitions, and if you've worked with them you know they deliver on them. We can choose the future skills we need in our ecosystem and recruit for those (coding, agile, lean, Design Thinking). We can choose the type of clients we want to work for (values-driven, innovative, social responsibility–driven) and the type of client contacts we want (human resources, business leaders, talent, new to role, experienced, and influencers). We can even choose to work with clients that we want to change from within—whether that be the overall client profile (for example, tobacco companies) or the type of role we want to deal with (change old mindsets in HR or in leaders).

Even in making friends, we have a choice. I witnessed a close personal friend making a racist remark. My immediate reaction was to decide to not be friends with them anymore—how could I live with my values and still be friends? It was only after a challenging and profound conversation with a client contact, Sean Boothman, that I changed my mind. As a black man who had suffered in this space, Sean persuaded me that it was better to remain friends and challenge my friend's attitudes from there—that was the tough but right route. Such a powerful moment for me as a leader and a person.

Once we have our buckets defined, we need to filter down the lists to a manageable level with a plan. To do this, use three simple questions: Whom do I need to delight in what I do? Whom do I need to satisfy in what I do? Whom do I just need to cooperate with? If you want to have more of a laser focus on this, then ask yourself: Who are the top three, five, or ten relationships to delight? These priorities will naturally change over time and need a constant review, but always being clear on which are the key relationships to delight and focusing your energy are essential.

Once you have them segmented, you have strategies to deal with each group. The Delight group gets a more comprehensive and tailored approach with a relationship strategy that includes investments of time, money, and effort. The second-level group, Satisfy, is made up of those who are critical to keep close but are in many ways either already advocates for you or are highly independent. They are normally people close to the delivery of key elements of your product or service. They are people you need to keep onside— but you already have a strong base of trust and engagement. They can, in some cases, be the teams that deliver service to the customers. They might be experienced team members who have a desire to be autonomous. On the client side, they are sometimes the buyer of the service with the clear message that if you are making their customers happy, you are delighting them.

The Cooperate With group has a different need. It is characterized by groups of people who, if not taken care of, could cause problems or blockages. They can include procurement, finance, and even learning and development people. They need a careful communication and contact strategy that satisfies them. This is where you have to make hard choices and adopt Juliet Funt's mindset of giving yourself "white space," meaning, the relationship is OK with "good is good enough."

The Trust Equation and *Sawubona*

Once you have made contact with those Delight and Satisfy groups, the next step is to build an effective level of trust. The basic elements of trust will be your track record (credibility) and your delivery on promises (reliability). What makes the real difference is the ability to build intimacy and reduce the levels of the feeling that it is all about what you want and not what they want (self-orientation). This is David Maister, Charles Green, and Robert Galford's Trust Equation:

$$\text{Trust} = \frac{\text{Credibility} + \text{Reliability} + \text{Intimacy}}{\text{Self-Orientation}}$$

One of the core skills in this area is based on *Sawubona*. This is a Zulu term meaning, simply, "I see you." The response to it is, *Sikhona* ("I am here"). This simple interaction is deeper than it first seems. It is about being truly present and listening with empathy to the whole person in front of you. It is the same skill that you will use as a design thinker in experimenting, as you take a human-centric observation approach to innovation—suspending judgment and truly listening. It will be what you use to make judgments in the Catalyst role as you coach and mentor. It will also be the skill you use in working out your presence stance and the appropriate version of connection.

In its simplest form, *Sawubona* is the ability to just be present and treat every encounter with someone as the most important thing for you. It sits within the levels of listening described in

Chapter 6, on refreshingly direct conversations. Every relationship is different. This means that empathic listening on your part at the start of any relationship is a key element in helping you enhance your understanding of the person, their reaction to you, and therefore your level of rapport with them. As mentioned earlier, referencing David Maister and colleagues and building trust, the level of intimacy required can be realized only by establishing deep rapport.

Empathic listening is the true sign of a great leader. A family friend who wrote for *Time* magazine said the most impressive person he ever interviewed was former US president Bill Clinton. He described Clinton's ability to make him feel as if he were the most important person in the world, and that nobody and nothing else mattered. He simply—but oh, how we wish it could be that simple—was totally present. He had a relationship with a purpose—and that purpose was the person he was talking to any one point in time.

Clinton lived that even if he disagreed with the person he was talking to. I recall watching him being interviewed by a theater audience via video link. In the middle of the session, he was repeatedly challenged by a woman because she did not agree with his response. She kept coming back with an argument. You could feel the audience's and the host's growing irritation with her. The host finally shut her down and moved on to the next question with a sense of forceful irritation. But the audience was still transfixed on the reflective and hunched figure of Bill Clinton. He had gone quiet and appeared to be in thought. As the next question was being asked, Clinton interrupted and said, "She's right!" With a long pause afterward, he then added, "Just because we might differ on the answer, she has the right to be heard. Let her be heard." He had listened, given her the credit, and she had her space. In effect, Clinton was saying, *"Sawubona!"* (I see you!) to the woman. The woman could have truly replied, *"Sikhona!"* (I am here).

The Long-Lasting Impact of Brief Encounters

Any relationship, or even just an encounter with someone, can have a long-lasting impact. In our business, we have many examples of chance encounters that have turned into either hiring decisions or sources of inspiration or recommendation. I recruited Stephen Buck, our platforms lead on our current team, while he was delivering a rental car to my home. It was not just about how he conducted himself on the drive to pick up the car with me; it was the way he made conversation with me and my daughters, and how he connected with us all. It was also about the conversation he hosted about my business, and the way he was curious. We swapped contact details and the rest is history. You never know when you will meet a future client or somebody you will end up working with. You should always engage anyone you meet warmly and with respect. It is always important to be present and truly see the person in front of you. You are always being noticed.

One morning, my colleague, Mike Taylor, and I met a woman in a hotel elevator in Hong Kong. She had obviously just been to the gym and confessed herself to be a "sweaty mess." We smiled and avoided making any untoward comment. I said, "You are just making me feel guilty I have not been to the gym yet." We parted at her floor and said our goodbyes with smiles. An hour later, we knocked on the locked door of a new client. The light switched on and the "sweaty mess" of a woman, immaculately dressed now, greeted us with the same smile. You never know who you will meet when and where, or how they will affect your life.

Showing curiosity and listening with empathy and patience are naturally easier with people you relate to and with whom you engage well. For those people you struggle with, this can be more challenging. It's tough to have a conversation with someone who, while useful to you in achieving your purpose, has an irritating way of engaging. It takes time to build your resilience and mindset to relate to them. That is why it needs to be combined with the next mindset.

Recruit for Growth, Not Fit

ExperiencePoint, which I mentioned above, brought me an idea that I love. They had just won a Business of the Year award and were telling their story. They said that most leaders and organizations recruit people to fit the culture. It seems right, and as we look at the research, we realize that we are attracted to people like us. However, the reality is that teams and organizations grow more effectively and keep themselves fresh by recruiting diversity and with growth in mind. The mantra they gave me that day is, "Recruit for growth."

Of course, recruiting for growth and difference is one thing; working with that difference and shaping a new culture is trickier. For every person who is different, there are many others who don't want to change or who see that difference as a threat. On top of that, there are many different dimensions to difference. Not every white, heterosexual male is the same. Not every person from a disadvantaged background will be the same. Not every logical thinker is the same. Not every front-foot person is the same. This topic could be a book or a life's work alone. The simple answer for the leader is about being conscious in recruiting difference and working to create the conditions in which that difference can thrive.

One important aspect of our definition of leadership, "agitating for the future," is that the leader's role is to have foresight about the different skills, mindsets, and behaviors that will be needed in the future. How they add that difference is a bit like a chef adding spice, testing the taste of the dish, and then adding more until the taste is right. The need for heat and stirring to make it into a dish falls under the role of the Host when they engage, which we will be looking at in depth soon.

Diversity = Profit

The fact that all organizations are driving toward a more diverse recruiting mix and inclusive way of working could be seen as driven by issues of gender, race, or age imbalance in the workplace, but that is now being added to by the work being done in Design Thinking and innovation. The Diversity = Profit equation is being proved by a large number of organizations in their work on innovation and product design. If your Fellowship of the Ring has three hobbits, a dwarf, an elf, an ageless man, a wizard, and a man, it's not just to tick diversity boxes, it's to ensure that all the different dimensions of this adventure are covered. And the team is not static; it grows, divides, and shrinks as required. Good guidance, counsel, and life-saving are delivered by different perspectives—female to male, elf to dwarf—and the quest cannot be completed without the unlikeliest (and most unliked) of team members: Gollum.

From the external point of view, on a simple level, our clients are from a diverse mix of backgrounds, genders, and ethnicities. If they see an organization that matches them, they are more likely to buy. But there are also other factors around value sets and actions matching values. Common values and acting by them are essential. That so many Airbnb owners now promote Lyft rather than Uber in their ads is a reflection on the Uber leadership and their treatment of gender. The days of hiding behind a brand label and packaging are gone. Social media and immediate feedback drives a higher moral standard, whether we like it or not. Connecting and engaging with those values and living by them is a business necessity.

A further compelling argument for inclusion involves the concept of extreme users. Design Thinking has proved that the pace and level of innovation is increased by observing extreme users of products or services. The fact that the end products will be sold to the middle, larger group of users in the bell curve does not stop us from looking for the outer edges of extreme users, who can have a significant impact on ideas. This also works in starting to shift your organization toward recruiting more people with different views and backgrounds. A great example of this is seen in IDEO's work with Bank of America. When looking at a niche group of single women with children, they noticed that the group rounded up when paying their bills and checks. Out of this simple observation came the Keep the Change banking product, such that Bank of America paid the exact amount to the supplier and put the rounded-up amount into a savings account for the customer. It was one of the most successful banking products, and popular across all groups of customers.

Your human ecosystem, network, and followers should be as diverse as possible to keep you sparky and relevant. Even connecting with people you vehemently disagree with or compete against brings ideas and vibrancy. I see the shift in inclusion in my own work and habits as a leader. Twenty years ago, I laughed at people who wanted to bring mindfulness and meditation into our work. Now I find that Headspace and meditation form a core part of clearing my mind, arriving fresh to challenges and a space where ideas come to me. Inclusion in recruitment and in listening to others' thoughts and views brings innovative ideas and success.

Rigor in Your Recruitment

As experts in recruitment, we have learned from our failures in the past. As the art of recruitment has progressed over decades, the certainty of recruitment decisions has increased. From the basic questions about who you are or where you went to school or who your father or mother was, we have moved to a more competency- and evidence-based interview process that asks for examples: "Give me an example of when you have faced a difficult client situation." This has, in the right hands, increased the predictability of recruiting successfully to a level of between 20 and 30 percent. But anybody can be taught to answer this type of question in an effective way and "pass."

The next level of recruitment predictability came with the invention of the assessment center. We use a half-day assessment process for our consultants. It requires the candidates to conduct real coaching sessions on us and handle client scenarios that we face or have faced. It is amazing how many people rate highly in a pre-interview but go on to fare poorly in the assessment. That does not make those people bad people or not right for other roles; it means that they are not a fit for the future skills, mindsets, and behaviors that I believe our business and followers need in order to grow.

We have about an overall 20 percent success rate for assessment centers—that is, only 20 percent of those who are asked to an assessment center are successful. That seems low. However, as in start-up businesses, we view a low success rate positively. We are being rigorous at maintaining standards! And yet it is still not a full guarantee of the success of those people in your team.

The ultimate assessment tool is to be able to see your potential followers in their real work environment being "natural." Without those observations and insights, you won't be able to predict their success and will continue to fail fast—and not in the way I support. The building of a network and habits and systems that get you out and about connecting with different people in action allows you to have that observation and insight. It also allows potential recruits to engage with you and see how you operate. Actively networking creates a healthy recruitment pool for your followers and your customers. The fact that ExperiencePoint attracts people to work with is balanced by an ability to see how those people work in the actual environment. If we want to really stretch ourselves, we have to take some risks on people. Risk mitigation for recruitment is about spending time connecting early through networking and observing. Or in real time creating experiments or prototypes around roles.

The Hard Part

The connection you make with people, and therefore the relationship you build with them, is crucial to your success as a leader. Whom you attract to your adventure and how they are attracted will be a mixture of your purpose oozing from every pore, how you treat them, and, most importantly, WIIFT (what's in it for them). They need to feel that they will be welcomed, valued, and able to contribute and grow. It is easy to hoodwink individuals for short-term recruitment. The regretted losses statistics show that keeping the right people is a more difficult task.

And however well you might relate with people, you can't take that as an indicator that they will relate well with each other. I remember as a teenager having two groups of friends: one from the school I went to and one from the area I lived in. Both groups of friends were amazing and shaped my playground as I grew up.

My naive desire was that, because I loved both sets of friends, they would get on well together. So I tried bringing them together... and I was disappointed. My connection with the one group did not seem to live as well as my connection with them as two separate groups.

Attracting and then engaging followers is about establishing habits, systems, and celebrations that breed and attract success. That's what we'll get to next.

So What? Connect

Suggested System: Pay It Forward

The first system I put in place as a business owner and consultant was a "pay it forward" system. The success comes from people playing the infinite game and gifting something to others with no expectation of a return. The system is based on identifying the key relationships and key gaps in your network. Once you have that analysis, you decide what you can pay it forward with. My strength is in mentoring and coaching. I frame my paying it forward to others in terms of my time and advice. My key differentiator is that I add "refreshingly direct" so people know exactly where they stand. What are you paying it forward with, and to whom?

Suggested Habits

1 Pay it forward: Start every relationship with the question, "What are the three things I can do for this person?" Explain to the person how you work.

2 Have relationships with a purpose: Make a habit of continually monitoring your relationships for purpose. What do you want from the focused group of relationships, and in particular what does each one give you?

3 Recruit for growth: Create a habit of looking for difference in your connections. Who could add significant challenge to your network and ideas? Where do you have gaps? Whom do you need to listen to, to understand your clients better?

Host: Engage

Say you have inherited a soccer team from the most successful manager ever, Alex Ferguson. You even got his blessing for the role. You have an amazing squad of players ready for the next phase in their career. You have been a successful manager in your own right. Surely it is just a case of walking in and taking over?

David Moyes, previously manager of Manchester United, now knows it is not that easy. Even with the right people, trying to engage a group of people, players, or functions and make them into a highly effective team is tough.

Sometimes people think it is easier for a leader who has a blank sheet of paper—no team and the choice of who they want to fill the roles. There are many start-up teams of failed businesses that could assure you, having a blank slate is difficult as well. The strike-out rate of start-ups is high. Investors know that. They would love to have a proven playbook for teams operating there. I wonder if such a playbook exists, and what it would look like. This book seeks to provide a framework for you to create your own playbook through experimentation, being more wrong, being more wrong again, and finding your own playbook for each scenario you face.

How do you build trust within this group of newly forming relationships to the point at which they actively wish to collaborate with each other toward the common purpose? More than just "forming, storming, and norming," it means holding a place of psychological safety, where individuals are able to create their own habits and systems, speak up, and feel they have enough freedom to be more wrong.

Moving from a group of individuals who are collected together or attracted together by a leader's purpose to an engaged and self-sustaining team is a tough step. The creation of habits and systems will help—the first of which is the very elementary "ritual sniffing"!

The engage phase is when the team or tribe start to "ritually sniff," as Jon Katzenbach and Douglas Smith write in their book, *The Wisdom of Teams*. This analogy from the animal kingdom is one that you—likely most people—might find distasteful. But it perfectly describes the first stage of engagement. The leader has brought the people together as a team. But as I highlighted earlier about my playground experiences, just because you value people as individuals doesn't mean they will get along. The key is to create a ritual sniffing environment in which to test whether or not the individuals will get along with each other. The ideal setup is one that is structured in projects and project teams.

In some cases, leaders are lucky and they bring together clusters of people who jell, without needing to implement a project-based culture. But even in that situation, cliques can form for various reasons. As experiments have proved, the first few people who join a team adopt a founder's mindset. Others who join later often feel at a disadvantage. They try to fit in rather than remain themselves, or they fight it and create their own cliques. The balance here for a leader is between giving the team the freedom to act and build their own culture and providing a sense of direction on the type of team the leader desires. The fact is, though, that the only way to get a team to a high sense of direction and a high freedom to act is to reduce freedom to act and give a strong sense of direction. That means that the engage phase is about the leader being willing to step in and lead the initial workouts they put the team through.

As any good personal trainer will tell you, if you want to build fitness, strength, and flexibility, you need to start with a rigorous workout plan. It involves a warm-up, a structured workout, and a cool-down for each session. It involves a longer-term plan that

builds slowly and begins with a strong core. It also involves looking at how you fuel those workouts, with sleep, diet, and hydration.
That is starting to sound like the Pi2 model.

Leaders need to start a training plan that drives fitness, strength,
and flexibility for the team. Like every good learning program, the
training plan for the team needs to be experiential. It needs clear
measures and content, and each stage of the program needs to be
run with a warm-up, structured content, and a clear review of learning. The team and individuals need to own their own learning. They
also need a guide—a mentor, coach, Energizer, Disruptor—someone
who provides a compelling purpose.

What's the Level of Risk You Are Willing to Take?

So how do you get your group to jell and start to work effectively?
Many leaders mistakenly define team success as members liking
each other and getting along. Don't get me wrong: that helps. But
the real measure of team success is the level of risk they are willing
to take, the psychological safety measure of feeling comfortable
enough to fail, and how quickly they become a self-energizing
entity—without the need for hands-on leadership.

The engage phase is the process of moving your team quickly
through the stages of forming, storming, norming, and performing.
This can be shaped by the values of the leader, but it's the leader's purpose, ideally, that keeps them engaged. Through the darker
moments, the team sees a light at the end of the tunnel. The True
North, or shared purpose, attracts them forward. In their minds,
they might have their own version of WIIFT (what's in it for them),
but the leader's purpose still provides heat and momentum.

We could spend the whole book looking at the dark arts of team
engagement and building. The "dark arts" is a term used when two
groups of eight players in rugby union football form a scrum, or
come together in tight formation, to win the ball when play stops.
How the players win the ball involves a variety of different factors
in bringing that many people into close proximity and trying to get
them to be effective together. Those dark arts depend on so many

factors that the more they practice and develop habits that are instinctive, the more they can adapt and be successful. The term "scrum" is now used for methodology in the agile community in start-ups—very apt for the challenge of bringing teams together, mastering the dark arts, and being wrong more often toward your purpose.

In the past, the use of sporting analogies for this was very popular. More recently, military examples have been used. General Stanley McChrystal's book *Team of Teams* is one of my favorites in this space. However, these are now being overtaken by some great business examples from the tech and start-up worlds. "Fail early, fail fast, and fail forward" plays a big part in team building. No doubt the investor's playbook mentioned above will attempt to formulate answers to such questions as: What are the habits, systems, celebrations, and conversations that will bring about the right chemistry and culture for team cohesion to happen? How can you, as Tom and David Kelley in their story of IDEO call it, get your team to "wing it like a start-up"? How can you use Ozan Varol's book *Think Like a Rocket Scientist* to bring a different thinking and exploring pattern? How can you apply L. David Marquet's "redwork/bluework" concept? Whatever you use, you need to have a mindset of risk and trying things you have never done before.

Although the above questions are only partially rhetorical, I find that the answers are best summed up in the anecdote—I love telling it—of a little girl who was in a drawing lesson. She was six, and she was at the back, drawing, and the teacher said this girl hardly ever paid attention, but in this drawing lesson, she did. The teacher was fascinated. She went over to her and said, "What are you drawing?" And the girl said, "I'm drawing a picture of God." And the teacher said, "But nobody knows what God looks like." And the girl said, "They will, in a minute."

As the leader, you can expect to find yourself in the position of that teacher. There's a questing element to the hero's journey; each path you choose could lead to solving a problem or to further problems, or make you turn back and try another path. For me, the key to the hero's journey, and to being more wrong, is that your followers become the heroes. They learn to be more wrong—to take risks and learn fast—and to achieve goals and learn from it all. Over the course of their journey, they have written and rewritten their very own playbook. Being strongly connected and engaged facilitates this—in all directions.

Your purpose as leader is not to know every answer to every problem—it is to decide which path to take and when you need to shift course to continue. The real problem-solving gets done by the team.

Project-Based Culture: OKRs and CFR as Habits and Systems

"It's been said that the five-year plan is dead." So wrote Salim Ismail in *Exponential Organizations*. By the time most plans are drawn up, the data they are based on has changed.

As I mentioned previously, the oldest model I have as a leadership consultant is the Leadership Paradox: that balance of providing a sense of direction for your team and giving them freedom to act. In the past, I was happiest and my teams were the most effective when we had a project to achieve in a limited time: The energy and camaraderie of completing a product launch at Procter & Gamble. The delivery of the most successful programs we ran for Barclays Internal Audit. They had some key things in common: they brought a variety of people together for a focused amount of time, with key deliverables, a significant challenge, and rigorous process.

That discipline of what a former colleague called our "operating rhythm" was made up of a number of important elements. It involved the regular daily drumbeat of communication. Churchill called his gatherings during the war "Daily Prayers." The rundown was: What did you do yesterday, what are you doing today, what are you doing tomorrow? Everybody, from the leader down, was involved. We call our team meetings our Daily Pulse, but it is the same concept. It allows us to keep an eye on alignment, areas of pressure, and any gaps that we have, and to act on that information. It allows us to laugh, share frustrations (the "bucket dump" mentioned earlier), and feel we are part of a ship that might be sailing rough seas but we have each other's backs.

Now, with technology, there are lists of different tools out there that create a structure to deliver this digitally. The advent of OKRs (objectives and key results) as a drill and mantra for teams is well documented. Individuals' ability to see a path between the organizational objectives for the week, month, and year and their OKRs provides alignment and transparency. The degree of transparency is important for the individuals and the wider team. It can show where alignment is off, where help is needed, and where others' work can contribute. That habitual, weekly discipline of sharing digitally is then backed up by conversations between team members and their leaders.

Much is written on the topic, but the book that captured my imagination most is *Measure What Matters* by John Doerr. Among other stories, he relates how Google used technology and digital sharing to build its success. He also talks about CFR (conversations, feedback, recognition). One of the biggest challenges organizations have had for many years is that of performance management—how to link performance and incentives. The answer is that pay and performance conversations should not be linked. Now, that is a much longer conversation and the subject of many books, so for now let's imagine that in this new project-based culture, the conversations on performance or progress are kept between the monitoring and discussion of OKRs and the use of this very effective CFR model. Another effective habit.

When you link back to being refreshingly direct, you can start to see where this all fits in. The CFR and OKR processes allow refreshingly direct conversations about progress and growth. Marquet's bluework (planning and idea creation), redwork (experimenting and action), bluework (review and reflection) pattern allows the same to happen. These are data-based conversations for which the data is provided by the individuals and measures in weekly real-time conversations. Recognition comes in the digital or verbal high-fives from team members and leaders. There may be celebration as well. Everybody can see what people are working on and how they are progressing. There is feedback on areas to improve. Most importantly, the drumbeat and rhythm is regular, consistent, and habitual.

Five-year plans in the leadership world are still being used at the boardroom level in many organizations. Below that, leaders need to adopt a project-based culture using OKRs and CFR to track and align the organization to their purpose. By setting your True North and aligning your followers with OKRs, they can ride the waves of change within an agreed framework of habits and systems.

The child in the art class is every member of your team. They need to find a way to release their potential by being more wrong. Their levels of ability to see through problems and reframe them as opportunities are boundless. You as the leader need to create the conditions for them to do that.

And one of the most important conditions you can create is that of psychological safety, so they can find ways primarily of learning fast with each other as a team.

Psychological Safety

Being able to speak up and say what you want can save lives, customers, and key people who would otherwise leave the organization or team. It can mean not wasting your time on work that is irrelevant or redundant. It can get you to shift your direction to take advantage of a change in the market or a client need. It can identify a problem in the figures that you may not have seen before. It can create a moment of customer "wow" that will live with them for a lifetime.

Amy Edmondson, author of *The Fearless Organization: Creating Psychological Safety in the Workplace for Learning, Innovation, and Growth*, labels this feeling that one can speak up without fear "psychological safety." She says, "In a workplace, psychological safety is the belief that the environment is safe for interpersonal risk-taking. People feel able to speak up when needed—with relevant ideas, questions, or concerns—without being shut down in a gratuitous way. Psychological safety is present when colleagues trust and respect each other and feel able, even obligated, to be candid." Adam Grant, an organizational psychologist, agrees. "Psychological safety is not: relaxing standards, feeling comfortable, being nice and agreeable, [and] giving unconditional praise," he says.

There is an amazing amount of work being put out there by authors such as Matthew Syed (*Black Box Thinking*) on how decision making and improving our capability in this area is about how we feel safe enough in teams to share our thoughts, ideas, failings. The principle is relevant in all areas of the Pi2 model, but where to put it in this book is an easy decision when you think about the meaning of "engage." How can people engage if they have fear that engaging is going to cause them pain, punishment, or loss of face? Being more wrong is essential, but it must be accompanied by learning from having been wrong, which means we have to admit we have been wrong, which means we need to feel safe to admit we have been wrong if we are to be truly powerful together. Psychological safety is part of the leader's contract with their human ecosystem. As leaders, we are fueled by a purpose that we help embed in our followers. With this fueling comes a desire to disrupt the landscape for growth. That comes with risk and, therefore, the culture we create in our teams needs to be one in which members feel they can take risks and also have open and rigorous conversations with each other when necessary.

Within an environment of psychological safety, your team will establish the necessary communication patterns for themselves—communication with you and with each other—in whatever form is appropriate, such as loops for giving and receiving feedback, having refreshingly direct conversations, briefback and checkback, team meetings, and team celebrations. In doing this, they create their own (and owned) habits and systems.

Let me use my own leadership, purpose, and team as an example. Leadership is not intrinsic to me but is defined by my followers. I drive my purpose through other people. Because my purpose for the business is "to create a measurable playground to disrupt the way people are led," I clearly need to create a culture that embodies the play aspect of the playground. The challenge is, how do I create a psychologically safe culture that takes risks, pushes the boundaries, makes mistakes, is self-sustaining, and allows my followers to be self-engaging with that culture? It's a paradox in that I would prefer for individuals to feel energized as if they are playing like children again—bounding into work, just like we bounded into the playground at school—but I need to be able to treat them as adults.

With his clients at Pheul, one of my contacts, Dean Gale, uses the idea of "renting" or "owning" one's role. If team members are renting, they're relying on others to maintain the fabric of that role, and they look for direction from their leaders. If they own their role, to quote an old expression, they "ask for forgiveness, not permission." This comes back to a leader's need for their people to have both a high degree of freedom and a strong sense of direction. Only through exploration and direct conversations can that happen. The rest we can "wing it with integrity" by shaping conversations toward a strong sense of direction and a high freedom to act.

There are going to be tough times, when my team members fall down and scrape their knees, when they fall out with each other and challenge my leadership. But I am not there to pick them up. I have their back, but they own their growth. Just as in the playground, the players establish their own habits and systems that let them learn, grow, innovate, and develop together. The leader provides the conditions that foster this, including psychological safety.

Titles and Their Impact on Engagement

All titles are seductive. They are the examples of the aforementioned given identities. You can slap a title or identity on your business card and hope that people use it to build the right image of you and what you stand for. In most cases, titles endow the bearer with a sense of where they might fit and what they might do in their organization. But what else do they achieve?

An example of the impact of this is illustrated by a team exercise I have been using in workshops for many years, called "Lego House." The group is split into two teams, called "managers" and "workers." Both teams are given instructions in separate rooms. In theory, they have a shared task of producing a building by the end of the exercise. However, as soon as they are given their label, either "manager" or "worker," they start to fit a stereotype. In reality they are all responsible. But consistently in this exercise, the "managers" spend hours developing their idea in their room while the "workers" sit next door doing nothing—waiting for instructions from the managers. Frequently, the workers end up "knocking off"—in one case, they even headed to the pub—while waiting for the managers to perfect the plan.

"Lego House" illustrates two points. The first is that if the managers had avoided the stereotype behind the label, identified that they were leading, and started connecting and prototyping earlier, they would have been more successful. Instead, they took a historical view of a label and fell straight into conforming to old practices. The second point is that individuals take a generic view of a label.

Everyone, to differing extents, hides behind their label or title: the managers in this case by not involving the workers in the design process, and the workers by not seeing the design as their responsibility. Instead of helping them organize and build, the titles actually held them all back. The titles neither predicted nor produced engagement.

The Trouble with Stepping Back
The dilemma I feel as a leader in trusting my team to get along and deliver is the same one I feel as a parent in allowing my kids to go out and have their own learning experiences. The tension that a leader feels is in how much they let their team go for it, how much they keep an eye on them and monitor their progress, and let them shape the future of the organization. I struggle with this in my organization. I tend to trust my team too much and give them a lot of latitude and space. That is a good thing for most people, but for some, it means that they struggle to craft their own direction. They are either very good at getting tasks done, or very good at planning those projects, or very good at communicating about their progress,

or very good at engaging with clients. Seldom are they very good at multiple dimensions.

So when I receive feedback from different parts of the team that they feel they are not getting time with me, I take this personally. That feedback is on all areas of my role or label as a leader—on communication, time in the office (virtual or not), coaching, not valuing them, not being clear enough, not having their back in arguments with their colleagues, giving them too much work, and so on. Each person in that team has their views on what has not been done for them and what I need to do better. As their leader, because I am human, I feel it is my responsibility to sort these issues. It is then that I start to grumble that I can never step back, that I never have the time to do what I need to do. It is their fault. I don't have the right people.

It is in this moment that knowing where your strengths lie is important—and that includes knowing where you don't have strength. This is especially when a leader needs a good support network around them. I could not step back unless I had my COO Sharon there to support the team. Stepping back is a term that, for a leader, does not mean disengaging. It means asking yourself: What conditions does the team need to be successful? It might be recruiting the right people to support them, putting the Daily Pulse in place, or making sure that the OKRs and CFR are alive and well. In the engage role, you are in a place of service. You need to be deeply connected to your followers and work out how to serve them in their unique and individual ways. I need to let my team make their own mistakes. My role is to put in place the leading indicators that predict whether we are on track to achieve our purpose. I need to find a way for the team to also own this measurement. They need to be hungry, humble, smart. They need to be connected and energized to deliver against those measures.

Nonperforming Teams

So that all sounds fine and dandy. But what happens when you inherit a team of poor performers and people who don't want to be there? What happens when you make a mistake with recruitment? What then?

This echoes a challenge that I hear more and more from leaders I coach and from other business founders and owners. It is driven by symptoms in their teams shown by individuals who they think want an easy life and for whom the work-life balance tilts more toward "life." I have a certain sympathy with this view as I reflect on some of my teams over the years. However, I must, as those other leaders must do, hold up my hands and admit that I was accountable for those individuals behaving the way they did. Insofar as I recruited them and led them, I had to take the plank out of my own eye before I could help them take the splinter out of theirs.

If you follow the logic of being more wrong, then you understand that 80 percent of your people that you or a previous leader in their role as Host have recruited will not work. They may be in the wrong room, they may be working in the wrong team, the team structure may not work—or, the big one: they may not be the right person. Being cruel to be kind is a core skill of the leader. You get paid to make the tough decisions. They won't like it and you will have a little bit of your soul go each time (that's how it feels to me). But when you see them thriving in another role later with another organization, it is a matter of remembering you were part of the reason their success happened—you let them go. (Be that as it may, you'd prefer this to happen at the earliest stages in the Pi2 cycle.)

Winging It with Integrity

As a leader, you have a duty of care. It is to "wing it with integrity"— which, as you may have noticed, is one of my favorite expressions. No leader can predict the future. That means we need to face uncertainty with resilience and integrity.

Defining "winging it" is easy: trying something with little planning or preparation. This is real life for most of us as leaders— remember, no plan survives first contact with the enemy. Some people argue that my love for winging it with integrity is mostly due to my lack of planning. I think there is some truth in that. By practicing winging it with integrity, I am purposefully practicing to face life as a leader and to be present. Allowing my team to be able to wing it with integrity with me is the skill.

"Integrity," however, is a difficult thing to define, particularly in different cultures and circumstances. My definition is one driven by the spirit of "pay it forward" and doing unto others as you would have them do unto you: integrity is about acting with a generosity of spirit—doing the right thing for others. The role of Host is summed up in this expression. It is about casting your net wide to build a human ecosystem that will populate the story toward your purpose. It is about allowing them to build their own way of working in a project framework. It is about stepping back but keeping an eye on the OKRs through CFR. It is about amplifying the team and individual voice through a culture of psychological safety and risk-taking.

So What? Engage

Suggested System: Create Your Own Role and Job Title

As a business owner, the riskiest system for me is based on giving authority to my team to craft their own roles and shape their own path. When you are recruiting a person at a very senior level and saying, "What do you see the role as?" you are taking a risk. Most people—such as my head of client development, Van Jennison—want at least a bullet point list of goals and objectives that my COO and I want from them. Once they have that, they need to do their own due diligence—their own crafting of the deliverables they need and the accountabilities they should have. But once they have done that, the role is theirs and they own and engage with it. Half the battle is won.

Suggested Habits

1   Focus on maintaining a clear sense of direction—for both yourself and others. The sense of direction is not the detail of what they will

do; it is the idea of what needs to be achieved and by when—for example, "We need the first prototype with the clients tested by the end of June." Being clear on that "sense" of direction toward your purpose provides clarity. It allows your team to go off and deliver without the need for you to micromanage them by telling them in detail what they should do. That is their role. Help them scope out an idea of success (and failure). Communicate what you don't want. Brief the team on how the action contributes to the purpose. Then let them fly.

2 Give them rope: Start with the premise that you are giving your people space to craft their own roles and then let them go. Just as we can't stop our kids from putting their fingers in a fire, we cannot stop our team from making mistakes. But that's the point—remember, this book is called *Be More Wrong*. That doesn't mean be more wrong everywhere all the time! It means to be more wrong in your "playground," where you are always connected and there to help others if they need it.

3 Run workouts to get the team going: Start every session, especially with new teams, with a warm-up workout. Drip-feed the experiences of what behaviors you expect. My favorite warm-up is Rock, Paper, Scissors, which we play in Design Thinking. Everyone pairs off and plays the best two of three. A reminder: rock beats scissors, scissors beats paper, and paper beats rock. Each winner plays another winner, until there are only two winners facing off against each other. The losers support the person who has beaten them, by chanting their name and cheering them on as they take on the next winner. This means that by the time they get to the final two playing each other, there are groups of cheering supporters for each person. The winner celebrates with everybody—the energy is amazing!

You can then explain that just like the game, the Design Thinking process starts with everybody having an equal chance to succeed. Just as with Design Thinking, not everybody wins, or has their idea taken on by the team. The losers have to let go of their ego and start to support the ideas or success of others. Design Thinking needs a process to work out what ideas are taken forward, because not every idea can be taken forward. Of course, the Design Thinking process is a bit more sophisticated than the game, but your team will get the point. Leaving egos at the door, focusing on just a few ideas, and supporting others are the key messages left with the group. With a strong buzz of energy!

8

energizer

RECENTLY, I WATCHED the seventh season of *The West Wing*: a show about a man running for president of the United States. It is compelling viewing and the pace of the storylines and incidents is frenetic. This season follows an election campaign that will take one of two candidates to the White House. Watching, I was most struck by the huge, unrelenting pressure the candidates were under and the stress it put on their people. The desire and need to not be seen as weak in any way or unable to cope with office, the constant fight through injury and a lack of downtime to "sharpen the saw," as Stephen Covey put it, are at the forefront. You can see the effect of this pressure in elected leaders and officials around the world: how they look when they are first elected and how rapidly they age.

Similar challenges face leaders in the military and sport—and leaders of businesses, no matter what size. The pressure on leaders is immense, whether it is the stress of watching cash flow or investment burn rates as they start up a business, or seeing donations to a charity dry up in the pandemic, or having clients pull work or contracts at a moment's notice because of the end-of-year desire to "hit the numbers." It is the pressure of leading people who have their own problems and challenges that affect the way they operate, and motivating them to perform at their best. "Running on empty" is a bad place to be!

Building and sustaining energy for both yourself and your team—that inner drive—is essential for success. To meet the challenge of all the leadership styles and maintain your energy—this is the essence of the Energizer. The hero needs to sustain a high level of energy to meet the rougher seas they and their team face. It is also their responsibility to chart a course and make sure the wind is in the sails, and to set the storyline their team will eagerly follow—in other words, to inspire. And it is their responsibility to ensure that they themselves remain fit to lead, mentally and physically, taking the needed time to replenish themselves. In doing so, they are building personal resilience and the ability to overcome the barriers to delivering the vision, as well as providing an example for their team—a strong energy and drive.

Energizer: Inspire

I am sitting down to think about which audiobook to listen to. My mind goes to two things. First, what story is going to inspire and energize me? Second, what is the voice reading it like?

When you're a leader, you're in charge of the stories that are streaming in to your teams and followers. You are in charge of the narrative and the storytelling that affects the mood and mindset of your people. It's your job to find what will inspire.

Inspiring through storytelling has always been fun for me, and listening to compelling stories is one of my passions. Learning from others' stories and then weaving them into my own stories has always been my way. Call it "stealing with integrity." When the stories are those of your followers, including your customers, and they feel part of your story, that is a double win. If you are leading your team on an adventure, a hero's journey, they need to be part of the story. It's up to you to find a way of creating a part in your story that looks fun for your followers. The key is in finding a way to weave the authentic you and your scenario, purpose, and followers into that newly crafted story.

As I've said throughout, being more wrong is about creating a playground for your human ecosystem. The challenge is to craft your story—or stories—about that playground experience, stories about great achievements, new ways of approaching the challenges you face, the dynamics of your team as they learn and grow, the unexpected heroes, the fight between good and evil. There are the triumphant failures that come from pitting yourself against the best of the best or against the seemingly insurmountable challenge. The stories of the followers and their highs and lows. You are bringing people together, helping and witnessing them grow, feeling that you have been a key part in their success.

When you are the Energizer, inspiring your followers takes up where the Host role left off by crafting a story around the purpose to generate action. In classic storytelling terms, it will involve chapters that build the characters and plotline. The jester or gleeman in stories had a repertoire of tales and songs of heroes that changed the world and inspired others to do the same. The quest for the Holy Grail, the first man on the moon, the first flight across the Atlantic, breaking the speed of sound, the invention of the Internet—all great stories. There's the story of Captain Tom Moore, who raised tens of millions of pounds to support the UK's National Health Service during the 2020 COVID-19 pandemic, and the stories of heroics in Chernobyl, of workers and miners sacrificing their lives for others to be safe.

Your story will have challenges to make it engaging and stretching. There will be guides, including you, who help the characters shape their own story and become the heroes of the leader's and their own stories. The narrative will be broken down to allow individuals to see their part in it and how they can develop to play their part in a way that is aligned with their authentic self. These are supporting characters, champions in their own right, as in the story of Steve Wozniak as the foil to Steve Jobs; Jony Ive as the designer behind the Apple domination; Michelle Obama inspiring millions in support of her husband, the president. They are the unlikely heroes, like the convicted criminal who saved lives on London Bridge during terrorist attacks.

As well as being aligned to the True North of the leader, the story provides direction for individuals so they know they are on course. It has clear measures of success or leading indicators that allow the heroes to measure their own progress. The key role of the Energizer—and, later, the Disruptor—is consciously taking a step forward as a leader and shaping the path for the followers to do as they are supposed to do: follow.

The reason people connect with stories is that they are a chain of cause and effect, with a beginning, a middle, and an end. The the journey within can be mapped and enjoyed, and the reader's imagination can take part in trying to work out the next chapters and the ending. In essence, this is the promise the leader makes as well. This is especially true when you adopt a "be more wrong" philosophy: what's coming next will be a surprise. You might be able to guess the next chapter, but as with all good stories, the one that is unexpected or unique captures the attention of the reader or the audience the most. In fact, if the next chapter is not unique and compelling, then the innovation levels are low and the story overall will not be compelling. We don't pay money to go to the movies not to be entertained and engage, whether that is to laugh, cry, feel anticipation or fear. Companies are not eulogized for average service or products. The fact is that part of "be more wrong" and leadership, in that spirit, is about the challenge and the delivery of the unexpected.

The story you are crafting as a leader needs to inspire your followers as well as yourself. You are the guide on a journey in which your followers can see their part and their ability to shape a unique and compelling role for themselves.

Lighting Fires in Bellies and under Backsides

Leaders are good at inspiring followers with their story, making each follower feel that their own story is being realized through their work for the organization. Leaders also push those followers out to fail fast and then hold them to account for it. This is "lighting fires in bellies and under backsides" in a nutshell. In some cases, the story told by the leader and the place the followers see for themselves in that story is enough to turn their own latent heat into fire—lighting fires in bellies. Most of us, though, need a jump start or a catalyst to get us going. We need some forward momentum from somebody else. If you have team members like this, you light a fire under their backside. Either way—belly or backside—a leader has a role to play in lighting fires. Once again, as the old analogy goes, you can't tickle yourself.

I have had many pleasant and unpleasant jump starts in my career, both consciously and subconsciously, from the people who have led me. One of my former managers, Rob Metcalfe, had a direct style that I liked. One time, he got feedback from a client that I had been working with: a session had gone very badly wrong. His approach was to find me in the office and ask me to come out to the parking lot. The parking lot "kicking" (my words) I received was a refreshingly direct conversation about preparation and reading your audience—coached and mentored until I got it. Rob was spot on, and the kick up the backside led to a renewed fire in the belly to never be knowingly underprepared in the future.

When I have received refreshingly direct feedback from a leader I respected, like Rob, I have kicked into life and made changes to how I operate. In other circumstances, it has been a stupid act on my part that has caused a leader I did not respect to deny me an opportunity I wanted. That also kicked me into life and started a fire. To refer back to Nassim Nicholas Taleb's book I mentioned earlier, the little bits of "poison" injected into our system are the fuel of growth, making us antifragile.

Both kinds of fires work, but the more self-sustaining kind is the one that is in the belly. Stories are a great way of bringing the fire to the bellies of your followers. A fire can make its way from your backside to your belly, too: Rob, in presenting the feedback from the client, shaped a vision of the future for me that was better. I could see my role in the story and had a desire to take part.

The "inspire" aspect of leadership is where the storyteller comes into their own. Your stories should inspire your team, or at least nudge them toward their own inspiration, which drives you and them to a shared purpose. Then, inspired by their role in the story, they can make their own mistakes and create their own "fail early, fail often, fail forward" chapters in their own hero's journey.

Every leader will find some of the styles described in Pi2 model easier to adopt than others. Telling stories comes more easily to me, but the ability to tell stories is in all of us. Just like other aspects leadership, it is a developable skill. I strongly believe that anyone can be a leader—but, as with becoming a top tennis player or sportsperson, it requires dedication, the development of helpful habits, and strong systems around you.

There are two parts to storytelling. You need to be able to create a good story, and also, as a famous UK comedian once said, "it's the way you tell 'em." Both parts can be developed. By now, it shouldn't be a surprise when I say that aligning your story involves purposeful practice and, of course, this takes time. Let me tell you about some of the most important things I bear in mind when crafting my stories.

Experiment with Storylines

Stretching into new spaces in your story takes practice. You work into them a little at a time. I see this as part of the playground, where you can experiment and develop an evolving style of leadership. I think of Steve Martin, a famously hard worker as a comedian. He would go to small clubs and play small gigs to test out his material before taking it on tour. In the same way, a leader crafting their "teachable points of view" should road-test their story and messages with a live audience. The story needs to evolve, and the message will have different iterations. Honing your message is a lifelong pursuit as a leader.

Crafting your use of voice and the structure of delivery of your message are essential. You can get away with a great message delivered in an average way and you can make an impact with an average message delivered in an outstanding way, but a great message with outstanding delivery is the goal. It takes practice.

Focus, Not Sprinkle

We have all read (or even told) stories in which new plotlines, multiple plotlines, or plot changes only distract rather than moving us toward our purpose. Only certain famous comedians can make a living out of being able to tell rambling stories and come back to a conclusion at the end. Ronnie Corbett was one of them; you are not. As a leader, you need laserlike focus to provide boundaries for the stories for your followers. In his book *A Promised Land*, Barack Obama talks about his early stump speeches that his advisor said "would pass him the test but not gain any more votes." It's more effective to present a few powerful stories and narratives than to dump a bucketload of stories that compete for brain space.

My COO Sharon Hardcastle and I constantly talk about "focus, not sprinkle." We attend a conference every year where our peers and competitors share their challenges and listen to experts on a variety of topics in running a business of our type. The consistent message that has been drummed into us by successful business owners is to clear clutter—and then focus. It is not about stopping things that are vital in the journey you are on; it is about how those things are completed, who completes them, and how you as leaders maintain a focus on what you need to do next. It is about deep work into a limited-focus area.

In his book *Deep Work*, Cal Newport shares a story that brings this to life for me and my business, and for all leaders. A farmer is looking at buying a hay baler so he can grow hay, bale it, and feed his cattle. After some detailed consideration—or, deep work—he realizes that while it may be what other farmers do, it doesn't make sense for him. Hay production is not his core area. He can outsource hay production—in other words, buy his hay from someone else—and he won't need the expensive baler, and not growing hay will allow his land to recover its fertility better. So instead, he uses the time he would have taken baling hay to rear broiler chickens to sell and make a profit.

It's a simple story, but the lesson is that we need to focus on our core purpose and direct our efforts to what we are good at.

At Potential Squared, we use partners such as ExperiencePoint (Design Thinking simulations), Sprintbase (Design Thinking digital platform), Everwise (learning experience platform), and Jenson8 (virtual reality experiences) to provide support for what we do not wish to specialize in. They are our providers of "hay," while we focus on what we are great at. Others have a part to play; bringing them in to play that part, at the right time, is a leader's role.

Collaboration is a sought-after skill, and state of being, in organizations. It needs to be a core part of your storytelling. This is borne out by the fact that collaboration is now embedded in the lean start-up movement, where outsourcing, buying in capability, or using shared tools is a highly regarded way of doing business. The practice of doing everything within your team or organization is out of date. Fit your partners into your story where they work best. Leveraging others through relationships with a purpose is important. So, focus your efforts—don't sprinkle.

Crafting the Story

You may be wondering how your leadership story should be crafted and then read by your followers or customers. How long a story should it be? The length of the story is not the main concern. Any story, whether it is a paragraph or a lengthy document, can be useful. Once you have the mindset that Donald Miller writes about in *Building a StoryBrand*, of ensuring the follower or the customer is the hero of your story, the next questions are: "How simple is the concept?"—if it is not, then make it simple—and "How compelling is the story for the reader or listener?" On that, you should be aiming for a rating of at least 8 out of 10.

Your next question is, "Who is your target reader?" This was a key question for this book you're reading now. I started with the assumption that it was the leader who is "stuck," but over time I realized that the readers I most needed to focus on were the ones who see themselves as an "unlikely leader." Whoever is reading the story will want to see something in it for them, so when I am crafting my story, I incorporate at least one teachable point of view.

Defining clear and testable "teachable points of view" is a tough part for me in storytelling as a leader. It was one of the first things I picked up as a leadership consultant, from Noel Tichy in his book *The Leadership Engine*. A teachable point of view is a way of working or behaving that has proved successful. One of my favorites is from one of my clients I mentioned earlier, Drew Cameron, who used to say, "When things are going well, go and tell your client. When things are going badly, run and tell your client!" It was a point of view that he embedded in every team he worked for. You could physically see his team running to be the first to tell the client when something went badly. The power of that was the trust that the client had that if something went wrong, they would first hear it from Drew or his team. Bad news is never good to hear, but it is escalated when you hear it from a third party. I have adopted this approach, this teachable point of view, with my clients. It is amazing, the trust you create.

The next question to answer as you craft the story is, "What's the authentic purpose behind the story?" Authentic purpose woven into a story is easier if you are writing for yourself. Crafting a story that hits the mark for other people's authentic purpose is more difficult. This is where focus and the Marmite effect comes in. Marmite is a vegetable extract product sold in the United Kingdom. It has a strong identity. The advertising premise is that you either love it or hate it. I describe my brand as a leader like Marmite—people either love or hate me. That's OK. Remember: leadership is not a popularity contest. As long as people respect you, you rate well. So your authentic, purpose-driven story should provoke a reaction. That reaction can be negative or positive, but it needs to register a significant score on either end of that scale. If they are speaking up about you, then there is a reaction and you are agitating for the future.

Finally, "Does it engage with those who connect?" The reader or listener is key, as are the circumstances. There are times when a short anecdote (think: elevator speech) is more appropriate and effective than the same content in a longer version told to colleagues on a social occasion. I find this approach in the emails I receive from bloggers such as Ozan Varol (*The Weekly Contrarian*) and James Clear (*Atomic Habits*). They give me a snippet of their overall story that I find compelling and sparks an idea in my head. The message is tailored to the medium (and vice versa).

It's the Way You Tell 'Em

We have already looked at the importance your identity and your presence bring to bear on your role as a leader, and we have stressed the importance of being authentic. It is this that will inspire and ultimately light the fires in bellies and under backsides. In the chapter on presence, I quoted Herminia Ibarra, who in a 2015 article in *Harvard Business Review* wrote, "By viewing ourselves as works in progress and evolving our professional identities through trial and error, we can develop a personal style that feels right to us and suits our organizations' changing needs."

So it is with how you tell your story. Telling stories is not reliant on charisma. So many leaders and excellent speakers I have seen have been understated in their delivery. But their words, passion, and attitude were authentic. You could tell that they believed the messages in their story, and their eyes lit up with different emotions they conveyed—just as the story you are telling must have your passion, purpose, and values woven into its fabric.

I always think about my stories, about my breakdown and failures. In those moments, as I tell people that I have failed, I need to connect to the feelings and the moments in my life that are authentic and also resonate with others. The story of me feeling not worthy to coach at a senior level; the story of me being incredibly nervous to speak in front of large audiences—even though I teach people how to develop presence as an executive; the story of failed business partners and how that has affected my confidence in myself. Those stories are best delivered from a place of humility and low prominence, in a reflective tone and style, not while standing in front of people, giving a polished performance. People really connect with you when your voice, tone, emotion, and words all match with the intent of your story. The most powerful instances occur when, in unscripted and emotional moments, people "come offstage" and bring themselves into the world of others. Being imperfect, making mistakes, and telling stories of vulnerability should be subject to the imperfect permissions of "be more wrong" to be true and authentic.

As a leader you need to find your own style to tell your stories. You can take courses to learn the structures that make good stories. You can learn about presence and dial up or dial down your prominence and gravitas. As Maya Angelou said, "At the end of the day people won't remember what you said or did, they will remember how you made them feel." You capture hearts and minds through the passion you have for your story and its impact. You will become a better storyteller with practice. The key thing is that unless the storyteller has the passion in their words and eyes, the story will be good but not outstanding—it will be heard but not listened to.

We can't match our story to every reader, but we can think in different genres and how the words and the characters might change depending on our target reader. And always, at the back of our minds, we are inspiring them to write their own story. Inspiring, helping, or nudging them at the right moment to go further.

Never did I think that I would write about the art of nudging. The only nudge I had experienced in my growing years was the "nudge, nudge, wink, wink—say no more!" of risqué comedies (Monty Python in particular). But many leaders now use the "nudge" as a way to get their team to stretch further and deliver at a higher level.

The nudge is on the same level as habits. Tiny Habits (tinyhabits .com) is a great website that teaches about breaking down changes you want to make. The author tells a story about being embarrassed, as an expert on habit, by being "told off" by his dentist for not flossing. He came up with the "tiny habit" of flossing just one tooth a day. When he did this, it seemed manageable, and once he had started with one tooth, he continued on to other teeth.

So it is with your storytelling as a leader: it is important to add a new chapter, plot twist, or character change in your story with just a gentle nudge. A nudge is nonthreatening yet still provides impetus in a certain direction so the team can carry on, with the majority of the momentum and energy, while remaining aligned.

Guiding your team forward to the True North might feel like herding cats sometimes. That usually means either that you have some elements of the ecosystem wrong—the True North, the story, the people—or that you are just hitting some turbulence. Dealing with the energy required to manage that is what we'll look at next.

So What? Inspire

Suggested System: Blog Your Life

The benefit in writing this book has been massive for me. The fact that it has taken me three years to write it does not worry me. The increasing value I have created by adding stories and rewriting sections has been worth it. Start journaling your days; start blogging your stories and views. You don't need a readership of thousands to make it worthwhile. By doing it on a regular basis, you are purposefully practicing being a better storyteller.

Suggested Habits

1 Test your storylines: Make it a habit to "visit the small clubs," as comedians do to hone their act. Choose people who will give you honest feedback on the impact of your messages and stories.

2 Focus, don't sprinkle: Create a regular habit of clearing out anything that doesn't align with your message and work priorities. Keep focused on a core set of messages and priorities for defined periods of time. As they say in *Top Gun*, "You never, never leave your wingman."

3 Give nudges: Create a habit of crafting small weekly nudges or messages to your people and followers. Keep them meaningful. Let people absorb and do something about them that week.

Energizer: Drive

I was sitting on a sofa in my parents' house in Newcastle, crying like a baby. I had finally realized that I couldn't cope. I needed help.

I was at the end of a journey that started with me leaving Arthur Andersen as they closed the office in Newcastle. I had been working as a tax consultant, completing handwritten calculations for personal tax returns, stuck in a cubicle and accounting for every six minutes of my time. I had the choice to leave and I took it, heading for a role at Procter & Gamble. The company name was strong in Newcastle, where its UK offices were. I was venturing into the world of pharmaceutical sales. I was excited to be joining a great company to be trained as a leader. My starting role was as a pharmaceutical representative, to learn the ropes. I hadn't figured out this work life yet: I now had a company car, was able to drive anywhere on weekends, and had money in my pocket, but the systems and habits I had were based on those I had learned and adopted at school and from my parents. I was winging this life. And I quickly realized that the life of a pharmaceutical representative was a soul-destroying one.

I was being asked to influence doctors to prescribe my products—if and when they saw a patient who fit the symptoms. I was rejected for more calls than I made with doctors. The life was one of dropping business cards, coming back later, and, more times than not, being told politely to go away. My answer to this slow drip of rejection was to go get a bar job in the evenings to try to find social connections in a city, Nottingham, I did not know. I was burning the candle at both ends. The icing on the cake was heading away to see friends in London and Newcastle to seek "warmth and friendship," not knowing that the effort that took was draining my energy even more. As I sat on my parents' sofa, my body and mind were giving me a reminder that my way of life could not continue. The tears were a symptom of that.

As I write this, I am having one hell of a week. I am struggling to keep my shit together. Yes, I am getting up every day, working out, doing Headspace, eating well, and at the moment have stopped chocolate ("That might be the problem," I hear you cry) and alcohol intake. So everything should be good, but it is a tough week. Still, I am a million miles away from that sofa moment. So what has changed?

Drive, in the context of the Pi2 model, means your personal drive and energy as a leader. It is about being fit to lead and a source of energy for your followers. A tired, confused, grumpy leader tends to lose followers. We all have bad days—and it is in these testing moments when you are having tough conversations with followers and clients that you need to find that fire and sense of inner drive and energy that will sustain your inspiration and forward momentum.

Building up that energy store to cope with the week I am having is not an overnight task. Having the personal resilience to stay focused and on track when all the world around you is under pressure and stress is hugely valuable. It takes a lifetime of purposeful practice to develop it. It requires introducing small amounts of stress and challenge into your life on a regular and managed basis so you become stronger. It requires systems and habits in your life that underpin that maintenance of resilience and energy. In James Clear's view, if you ever think you have this cracked, then you have missed the point.

So Why Do You Need This Energy?
The Cost of Being More Wrong

The central premise of being more wrong, of failing fast, is that you fail earlier, more often, and forward (in the direction toward your purpose). Your purpose is your reason to leave the path that you have trodden for so long. No one said it would be easy—and in fact it is always challenging to be more wrong. Many times you have to sit and listen to people blame you for mistakes. Your people need a lot of time and reassurance as they struggle to deal with ambiguity. Your customers trust you but, even having bought into your central premise, may still need your support to defend those mistakes elsewhere in their organization. This might be the hundredth time this week that you have failed. You are fighting against a natural reaction to see failure as a problem. As a leader, you need to fortify yourself to hack your way through the thickets and climb the hills. Your fortification is about your energy and resilience.

Taking a different path, particularly if you have been successful on the current one or have invested a lot of resources in one direction for a long time, is a tough decision. You want to know if the new direction is the right direction. You want to know if getting rid of twenty products and focusing on one product is the right move. You want to know that moving from a controlling style of leadership to giving people space to express themselves will work. But you don't know, and you could become paralyzed by the enormity of the consequences of being wrong. However—and this is where we make a judicious choice—if we start to live our life as a series of experiments that are quick, low-risk, and very low cost, we can start to find out the answers without losing our shirt. We will explore this principle of experiments in depth as part of the Disruptor style. This chapter's focus is on energy and resilience.

Fit to Lead—Resilient to Lead

To have drive and energy as a leader, you need to take responsibility to ensure that you are, literally, fit to lead—mentally (for example, through meditation) and physically (for example, with exercise, nutrition, and sleep)—and taking time to replenish yourself. In doing so, you are building personal resilience and the ability to overcome the barriers to delivering the vision, as well as role-modeling for your team.

The term "fit to lead" has been in the industry for a long time, in many different versions. There is a large body of work on physical fitness and how to use exercise beneficially, whether that be walking, HIIT (high-intensity interval training), weight training, running, triathlons, yoga, or swimming. On top of that, there is the work on mental health and fitness. The ability for a leader to maintain a healthy mind and also deal with mental health issues is key. But there is still a stigma around mental health. As someone who had a breakdown in my late twenties and who still suffers from anxiety, I have become transparent about sharing my suffering and how I manage that now. It is amazing how many others can relate and have their own battles they are fighting. Sharing and vulnerability allows a leader to build trust in their teams and encourage them to share their own concerns or problems.

One further, sometimes overlooked, area is spiritual health. While most organizations now accept physical and mental health as factors they should pay attention to, spiritual health is part of the more contentious group of factors that either is not mentioned or is ruled out for discussion by different countries, cultures, and geographies. "Spiritual," for me, is about belief systems in general, including religious, political, and cultural beliefs. I grew up with a grandfather who was a professor of theology and a Church of Scotland minister, and I have been privileged to sit and listen to many people who have shaped my view of my belief system. I have formed my own system of beliefs that have been influenced by my experiences. They continue to be shaped as I experience being a father, husband, son, friend, and leader.

I have grown to see this central concept of being "fit to lead" within the context of overall mental, physical, and spiritual health, the different dimensions of which need to be shaped on an individual level as a leader. We must remember that leadership is a journey and that the leader needs to model the ability to make that journey in a sustainable way while also supporting others. To work on your inner drive, you have to start by looking after yourself and learning to become "properly selfish."

What does "properly selfish" mean? The example I carry with me, told to me by a colleague, is of a group of marines sent to help in an earthquake-ravaged city. Each night they would return to their base after helping the sick, injured, and suffering and sit down at a table full of food. Their faces were long and sad, and their chaplain eventually asked what was bothering them. They said that they had been dealing every day with people who were starving and dying—surely they should be sharing this food with them? The chaplain paused and then asked them, "Who's going to look after them when you are sick?" If they didn't properly nourish themselves, then their energy as leaders in the field would be diminished.

In certain belief systems, selfishness has always been seen as a negative characteristic, much in the same as being a "victim" has been (in other words, blaming others for everything wrong in your life), or being prideful, or as is expressed in the warning, "excess of anything will lead to illness or pain." I have come to realize since my childhood that some of these beliefs are enabling and some are disabling.

As a parent, there is one concept of being "properly selfish" I can buy into and live: It is unhelpful to put our own lives on hold until our kids grow up. That sounds sensible, but many people subjugate their needs to those of their children. What that says to your children is that nothing happens for you or your career while you are doing the parenting thing. You come to believe that you should not go for a run, have an extra hour in bed, or meditate, because that is selfish. It can lead to the idea that it is selfish to take time away from being a parent or leader to recover or even think.

The truth is that using others as the reason for not taking time to look after yourself is avoiding the bigger issue that in all probability is apparent to and unspoken by everyone who comes into contact with you. If you want to be a role model for your children, your followers, and others, you cannot wait for the ideal conditions and make excuses. As a leader, father, friend, and colleague, I need to work out the enabling beliefs to help me find a properly selfish way of taking care of myself. It is then that I can develop an antifragile mentality and fitness that enhance my energy and presence in my daily interactions. I want to ensure, above all, that I remain fit to lead and will not, at the critical time, run out of mental or physical energy.

Being able to work on yourself for the benefit of others and toward an amazing purpose that benefits others, like the marines I mentioned earlier, is the ultimate goal. Taking time out to rest, to do deep work individually, is not selfish if it helps you be fit to lead and is in the service of delivering for the bigger purpose. And operating at your intellectual optimum has to be supported by physical well-being.

The SHED Method outlined by performance coach Sara Milne Rowe is just one way of describing the array of effects on our ability to lead or just generally deal with life successfully. SHED stands for sleep, hydration, exercise, and diet: the four dynamics on which she provides guidance for her readers. The fact that everybody is different is important. Each individual leader has different needs. I need eight hours of sleep a night to function. I try not to work on weekends. I need a blowout or party every so often to let off steam and keep myself sane. What some people call "cheat days" are an important addition so that you don't feel you are totally denying yourself everything you like. At the other end of the spectrum, I have a number of colleagues who survive on two to four hours of sleep— not by choice but because of sleep issues. I know people who work seven days a week and find that type of life energizes them. This is not about what works for all. This is about you making choices about what works for you, your body, your life, and your passions.

I can't advocate strongly enough for regularly taking time out and off from work, though. One of the first strategies I learned when I joined Procter & Gamble was Stephen Covey's habit of "sharpening the saw." In his book *The 7 Habits of Highly Effective People*, Covey based this habit on the fact that most people—including leaders—forget that they have an exhaustible resource of energy, whether that be physical, emotional, or mental. If you can take time from cutting trees to step back and sharpen your saw, you will be more effective. You can't just keep on sawing down trees when your tool becomes blunt. Taking time out to sharpen that saw brings you back fresher and more effective.

A few years ago, I would have scoffed at the idea that meditation could fit into my life. If you don't already meditate, you may well be feeling the same now as I did then. But experience has taught me that a mind full of information, stress, and pressures needs to have a habit within a system that allows the individual to fall out of their own thinking. We all know that our best ideas come when we are switched off—in the shower, on a run, even asleep. We need to find a way of creating that space in our daily lives, not only so we can find those best ideas but also so we can continue to think clearly and have the bandwidth for challenges. Only when we take mental breaks to interrupt the flow of overdrive can we be resilient and consistently effective in our decision making.

Nowadays, there are all kinds of names and apps for basically the same idea—Calm, Headspace, meditation, emotional space— of taking time for yourself to recalibrate, take stock, or just spend a few moments doing nothing at all. This is part of being properly selfish too. But I'm not out to convert you. You need to step into the playground of the Energizer and find your own path to spiritual, mental, and physical health. You know you need it as a leader. The only question is finding the best option for you.

So, by being fit to lead, you are physically, mentally, and spiritually set up to encounter and embrace the daily and long-term challenges of leading.

Fit and Resilient Followers

Never underestimate the impact of modeling these habits and systems wherever you are. You can easily reinforce for your followers the practice of looking after oneself for better performance by doing what you can to ensure their physical and mental well-being. Organizations are recognizing the benefits of supporting their workers' overall health: IDEO, the largest design agency in the world, is a leader in innovation but it also internally practices what it preaches with its people. The fact that they have a director of space whose sole role is to create a balanced workplace for the organization says it all. Not only do they have places to nap, but they also have an IT help desk that during the day is also a cafe and at night turns itself into a bar. You can get your laptop's problems sorted out while you relax.

Many leaders and organizations have trust issues around providing an environment in which people can relax, reflect, reenergize, and do their best work. Working from home is a classic example of this, with some organizations claiming that as much as 30 percent of their organization is working from home. But do they trust their people to work effectively at home? And how do they measure effectiveness? For example, does less log-on time actually mean being less effective? There are many ways of looking at effective work. A lot of us are busy fools, but are we effective?

Now, at the time of writing, we are working in a way enforced on us by a global pandemic. We have found that in reality many people are more productive at home. Organizations are starting to plan for working from home. However, the underlying issues of working from home can be significant for many. For example, those whose home space is limited have found they are working from their bedroom—or worse. (A design award was even given to someone who constructed a desk/ironing board combination to save space in their limited workspace.) Reduced social contact because of working from home has also raised an issue, concerning mental health. So the jury is still out, but there are positive signs that decreased commute time, more workout time, and an increase in family time are major benefits for individuals.

Organizations cannot watch their people all the time—and they shouldn't try. Trust is the basis of the relationship between leader and team. Disallowing working from home because log-on time is at 35 percent is saying, "I don't trust you." I do struggle with trusting my people and giving them space to perform and work as they want to. I have had my fingers burned by people taking advantage of the freedom that I have given them. But the more I experience this issue within my business and other organizations, the more I realize that one of the underlying causes of negative results from providing freedom has been the mismatch between my purpose and theirs. I am not saying that everyone's purpose should be the same, only that work needs to be done to align workers' purpose with that of the leader and organization. When there is poor alignment, the individual is using their energy reserves to maintain a false engagement level. A purpose everyone is aligned with creates enough heat to fire the initial energy needed and for it to be self-igniting as people continue down the path.

There is also the power of focus, fostered best by having shorter, more focused work sessions. Some research shows that people should work in ninety-minute slots, taking breaks in between. Efficiency is massively improved by this rhythm of work. How much more productive would someone be if they could work not just in shorter sessions but when their natural rhythm lets them be more effective? For some it might be a 4:30 a.m. start; for others, it is working from home. It could be formal attire in the office for some, or jeans and a T-shirt for me. What is it for you? More importantly, what is it for people who work for you?

We now live in the age of technology when virtual working brings significant new options and also new challenges, and even if we are reluctant to take full advantage of them, the worldwide pandemic has obliged us to. Enabling and encouraging your followers to work out their own rhythms, habits, and systems using purposeful practice to create a new and sustainable energy should be among your first steps toward building fitness and resilience for your voyage.

The energy you have through being fit in body, mind, and soul will complement the energy you have from knowing your purpose, your True North. Together, they increase your and your followers' resilience to setbacks. They increase your ability to be clear under pressure. As a resource, some of this energy will necessarily be used in overcoming the failures and obstacles you will encounter in your journey of being more wrong.

The Resilience to Be More Wrong

As an element of the Energizer leadership style, drive is asking for a lot of trust and bravery from your followers. Failure and being more wrong are becoming more embedded and, as we shall soon see, are going to increase. So it is important to build resilience in yourself and your followers for both the present and the future.

To take action confidently and be wrong is conceptually easy to understand, but it's much harder to realize in practice because failing is scary, and getting back up again can be hard—and sometimes embarrassing. Failing early, failing often, and failing forward require great resilience, at both a personal and a team level. And unfortunately, while resilience is an integral element of being fit to lead, it is rarely given its proportionate amount of air time.

So how do we create that "OK-ness" with being wrong? How do we get onto the front foot when it seems scary and we have only 30 percent of the data to make that decision? The first step is to remember that you need to look to others for help. This can take many forms—for example, I read, listen to podcasts, attend conferences and seminars, and draw inspiration from current and past leaders. It is for this reason that I have an advisory board of three mentors and a coach of my own. I also adhere to the principle of experiments that encourages OK-ness with being wrong.

Let's take a look at some of my helpers in building and sustaining resilience.

Examine Your Programming (and Your Mindset)

I don't know about you, but neither my parents nor my school ever celebrated 20 percent as success. Our upbringing has programmed us to avoid failure. Worse, we've been raised to prize success as the opposite of failure. For many people, being wrong is not a position of strength. But maybe, like the little girl who was drawing God in her art class, we are being evaluated against the wrong measures. I am constantly amazed by how people I coach continue to hold to measures of success that are other people's and not their own. Like the drunken man I mentioned at the beginning of this book, they are looking to find the keys under a light, but the light is not shining where the keys are. To achieve resilience you need to be clear about your own measures of success. And we have seen how this evolves when you're establishing your purpose. That's why I talk about exercising and stretching into different spaces.

Another metaphor I often come back to is of taking small amounts of poison to build tolerance. This is as true for individuals as it is for developing and supporting a group dynamic through the innovation process. You don't need to bite off more than you can chew; this is about process—the journey. Small failures that are achieved with a focus on learning are the mantra of start-up organizations. Success rates of 20 percent in start-ups are celebrated as part of a journey toward success. So I've gotten new programming: 20 percent has been reframed, and I can see that success comes from failing 80 percent of the time.

Challenge (Bad) Habits and Experiment with New Ones

Peter and Jane have invited Jane's family for Sunday lunch. They've got a lovely cut of beef to roast, which Jane prepares while Peter sorts out the vegetables. At one point, Peter looks over. "Why are you cutting the ends off the beef?" he asks.

"It's what my father always does," she says. "I don't know why. I think it's because it makes the meat more tender."

Once it's all in the oven, they go and join the group in the living room. Peter asks Jane's father why he cuts the ends off the beef. "It makes the joint cook faster," Jane's father says. "It's what your grandmother always did."

So Jane turns to her grandmother. "How did you learn to cut the ends off the beef before you roast it, Gran?" Her grandmother looks up from playing with her great-grandchild. "Cut the ends off? I haven't done that since we bought a bigger oven!"

We all have various things we do just because we've always done them or because other people do them. They've become the things we take for granted, whether they're helping us or not. But you can't improve the way you do things if you don't question why you're doing them.

Interrogating your own practice—the way you and your team have done things for so long that you'd say you've always done them that way—can shine a light into dark corners. Sometimes it is obvious where change needs to happen, and it may not even take a process of innovation to achieve it. Sometimes it's more of a challenge.

When you can't see what's wrong and when there is no obvious answer, innovation comes into play. You start with rigorous observations and empathic listening with nonjudgmental questions. You can choose to hide behind your habitual actions—after all, this is taking refuge in what you can say you know—or you can look for the things that you don't question, the things that perhaps you don't even see, and start working on them toward growth.

Other habits don't offer tangible gains, and some, like smoking, eating too much, and procrastinating, we actively struggle against. Yet more habits, such as how we respond to acute stress, can be completely invisible to us, even though others see them clearly in us. Ignorance is not bliss—if we don't recognize these habits, their impact can even be more destructive, since they lead us to act without considering how our actions align with our intended outcome.

I remember a story of a junior finance employee who took it upon himself to fill a huge boardroom table with all the reports that the finance team produced for their business in a month. He invited the finance team in and started by throwing in the bin all the reports that were duplicated somewhere else. With that, 50 percent of the reports were gone. Then he picked up all the reports that clients said they did not value anymore and threw them in the bin. By the time he had finished, he had removed 70 percent of the original reports. A new day had begun in that finance department and a large amount of "reporting" work time could now be shifted to insight and true business partnering. The lift in frustration and stress about being report writers was palpable.

The purpose of the drive stage is to move to action. Moving to change the ways you work by removing bad habits is a great place to start. However, there is also value in experimenting with new behaviors. Herminia Ibarra comments, "Without the benefit of what I call outsight—the valuable external perspective we get from experimenting with new leadership behaviors—habitual patterns of thought and action fence us in. To begin thinking like leaders, we must first act: plunge ourselves into new projects and activities, interact with very different kinds of people, and experiment with new ways of getting things done. Especially in times of transition and uncertainty, thinking and introspection should follow experience—not vice versa. Action changes who we are and what we believe is worth doing."

This fits well with my view of leadership being about sailing your ship out of the harbor and seeking rough seas to stretch yourself and your team. L. David Marquet's distinction between bluework (reflection) and redwork (action) is useful here: Stretch yourself and the team to work on the edge and to different pressures (redwork). Then return to the harbor to reflect, replenish, and work out what is next (bluework).

Jamie Smart, author of *Clarity*, sees reflection as the most underutilized skill in leadership. In our desire to be "driven achievers," we must remember that time to fall out of our thinking and reflect (bluework) is important. Smart encourages individuals in his three-day intensives to do deep work (redwork) for ninety minutes to two hours and then go off and do other things (bluework) for ninety minutes. We will look at this more fully in the chapter on the Catalyst role. The key point right now is that, although it might sound counter-intuitive, the more I seek reflection time as a leader, the more effective I become.

Develop a Growth Mindset

We all have it in us to be our own worst enemies. Holding ourselves accountable is part of being an adult, part of striving for the best and to keep becoming better versions of ourselves. And if you are like me, then you will have a little voice, the inner critic, that keeps beating yourself up. Particularly in times of stress, my inner critic will create a list of all the things I did wrong . . . and not in a healthy way.

There's no way around it: failure is personally taxing. Just as successes bolsters teams and send them out celebrating, so failures precipitate the hard work of deriving insights and working out what to do differently next time. Obviously, the trick is to see this as a good thing. Sometimes it's easier said than done. In his book *MindStore*, Jack Black gives a mantra about reframing. His example is of how often we hear ourselves say, "I'm tired." The impact of that statement on us and others is negative. The source of the answer to that is, "I need more energy!" Now, that is easier to deal with. Off for a walk, a coffee, a nap—or to call it a day.

If a key feature of resilience is to see failure as a good thing, and promote that mentality through teams, then that acceptance needs to start at home. This is helped by the concepts in Design Thinking. Framing a problem statement with "How might we...?" allows us to be more creative, which will open up even more avenues. Carol Dweck's book *Mindset: The New Psychology of Success* talks about the difference between a growth and a fixed mindset. In her research, the ability to see failure as a way of learning and growth distinguishes people who are going to be more resilient and ultimately more successful.

You Are the Role Model!

There is a time for settling into high-intensity work mode to just get things done. There are also plenty of times when, as mentioned earlier, a leader slips into "driven achiever" mode (lots of hard work but no clarity of why they are doing it) without noticing. The fact that we need to be role models and lead means that in many cases we need to be the person who provides the drive, the one who sets the pace. The clear distinction that we are making here is that drive is not about driving others—as in a bus. It is about personal drive that oozes out of every pore and is infectious to those around us. When you see leaders in the mode of flow, who know why they are driven and what they are driving toward, they look like they are cruising through the rougher seas. They seem unflappable. Nothing seems to faze them. They are not just working harder—that's an illusion. These leaders are in that zone through inside-out thinking, purposeful practice, and having taken care of their physical and mental well-being. Ask Novak Djokovic as he sits astride the tennis world. Ask Richard Branson as he sits astride Virgin businesses. They will tell you their stories of systems, habits, and purposeful practice, and how those all contributed to their resilience.

You and your followers are now Energizers—inspired, with the drive to act and the resilience to face failure. How you and they act is covered next, when we talk about the Disruptor.

So What? Drive

Suggested System: The Beginning of the Day

My biggest change to my life is in how I start my day. I have crafted a system of habits that sets me up to be my best version of myself for the day. No matter the day of the week, even Christmas and my birthday, I start it the same way:

1   I begin with a workout, bike, walk, or HIIT session.

2   Then I stretch right after the exercise, focusing on flexibility in my back and hips.

3   Next, I do twenty minutes of my Headspace practice.

4   After, I lie on my back with a heated beanbag over my eyes to rest and massage them, and while in that position, I do ten minutes of Pilates. At the same time, I also explore new music.

5   After all of that, I have breakfast and coffee while filling out my habit tracker and journal and writing down the three things I am prioritizing that day.

This system of daily habits energizes my mind and body and fuels my brain for the day ahead.

Suggested Habits

1   Use Headspace: This is the one habit that has transformed my mental health and effectiveness as a leader for the better. No matter the mindset I have going into the twenty minutes, I come out with a clear head, and in many cases answers to some of my challenges. The trick is consistency: I do this every day. It is an infinite game for the mind to keep it healthy.

2   Sleep: There are so many books written about sleep. My good friend Giles Watkins has written one, *Positive Sleep*. Its holistic approach

is a great one to take. So much impacts our sleep. I have a habit of going to bed no later than 10 p.m.—or, if I am lucky, by 9:15. I read before bed on a Kindle with subdued lighting. I try to avoid the phone an hour before bed. The key habit for me is to get at least eight hours of sleep a night. The body needs rest and it needs routine to add to the power of that rest.

3   Stretch: Our body tells us when there is something wrong with us. It has systems that send messages, whether they are headaches for dehydration or muscle pulls for overdoing exercise. The aim here is to take care of your system. I have to sit a lot, so stretching, plus doing Pilates at the same time, strengthens my physicality for the strains of leadership and life.

9

disruptor

'M SURE YOU know that Henry Ford disrupted the world with
the Model T by crafting a new way of production and a new
form of automobile that radically changed the car market and
stole a march on his competitors. Did you also know that his world
in turn was disrupted? When consumer interest changed, the Ford
approach became obsolete. He had to shut down his production
line for a considerable amount of time while he tried to change his
approach. In that time, General Motors stole the market.

What did Ford miss? He was focused on making a consistent
product at a low price, but the market was looking at buying not on
price but on a new view: a changing version of model every year. By
presenting new versions of their models each year, General Motors
stole a huge market share. Ford could not adapt to that way of producing cars without a lengthy shutdown.

As I've said before, leaders need to disrupt themselves before
others do it for them—when they are most comfortable and when
they least want to: at the top of their game.

If you are of a certain age, like me, there was a time when you
thought your prized LP or CD collection would last forever. You
never considered that you'd end up packing that collection into
boxes and storing them in the garage and instead selecting your
music from digital downloads on a platform called Spotify. You

probably didn't even think you might want to do something like that. Steve Jobs at Apple did. He had a vision of music being stored digitally. First, he launched the iPod. Do you remember that at its launch it was panned by the critics? Jobs was not bothered. The first steps had been taken on the journey toward iTunes, digitally storing your music, and then music streaming. Jobs had his eye on the longer-term prize. He was willing for his product to be perceived as not perfect—to "fail ugly." His goal was to bring iTunes to the fore and, in the longer term, the iPhone would be the better version of the iPod as a streaming device. That spirit of disruption keeps Apple at the top of their market.

These stories illuminate a specific aspect of the need to disrupt: You can never be complacent. If you are at the top of the game, you need to disrupt yourself before others do. If you are playing the "long game" to create a radical, new, and unimagined product, as leader, you need to embrace your inner or hidden Disruptor. The leader as Disruptor has two main responsibilities: to experiment and challenge.

Experimenting, in its simple form, is creating a playground in which you are conducting a constant series of experiments to enhance the approaches you use and the products and services you deliver. It draws on the current trends in Design Thinking, agile methodology, lean start-up, and decision making. As a leader, you are seeking to create a culture of innovation. Creating a playground where you can be more wrong is essential to this culture.

Once you have that playground, you need to then apply the concept behind "challenge" to know when you have been successful and when to cut your losses on an experiment. Living in Disruptor mode is about the ability to hold that tension between experimenting and cutting losses to move on when things do not work. That tension and that ability is a key differentiator in the Pi2 model.

Disruptor: Experiment

The definition we at Pi2 use for leadership is "agitating for the future": the art of future-proofing your organization. How can you peek around the corner and see what is coming? Some people try to guess based on what they've already passed. But as Nassim Nicholas Taleb says in *Antifragile*, it is impossible to accurately predict what will come in the future from what we have seen in the past. Instead, we have to be prepared for what we can't see by ensuring that both the systems we have and our people are antifragile—more resilient so we can successfully ride the waves of change in the future. We have looked at some of that in the previous chapter, on the leader as Energizer. For the Disruptor in particular, Design Thinking is one of the tools leaders can use to apply a growth mindset to the future and craft products, solutions, or ways of working that go beyond simple extrapolation, past the obvious ideas, and to make breakthroughs. Henry Ford may not have actually said, "If I had asked my customers what they wanted, they would have said faster horses," but if he didn't, he should have.

Creating a unique edge or difference in your approach, product, or service requires unbiased human-centered observation to unlock ways of meeting as yet unarticulated but nascent needs. The example I love—which I've already mentioned briefly in connection with the Host style of leadership—is about a piece of work commissioned by Bank of America and completed by IDEO. The original brief was targeted at how they might get more people to open bank accounts. The team followed families, and in particular mothers, as they went about their day. By seeking extreme users, in this case single mothers, they identified a trend: single mothers tended to round up their checks to pay bills. So if the bill was $27.40, they rounded it up to $30.00. That observation led to the insight that people rounded up bills for peace of mind and to get ahead of their debts. The idea that was put in place as a result was that Bank of America would pay the $27.40 and put the difference between that and the $30.00 into a savings account for the customer. The

"Keep the Change" banking product was one of the most successful banking products ever—so much so that when they tried to remove it years later, there was an outcry.

Another example I'll remind you of is that of Sir Dave Brailsford, who has driven success in cycling with incremental changes to give his teams the edge, from innovating the type of pillows and the fueling system for the riders to having separate washing machines for each rider. They are constantly experimenting to shape the future edge in the sport.

Shaping the market or sector through differentiation in product, service, or ways of operating is essential. Standing still gets you nowhere fast. Often, this Disruptor approach focuses on radically new ideas, but much innovative thinking and many solutions are those small, incremental changes we just talked about: they make life easier, and you always wonder how nobody had thought of them before. Even being able to iterate the human interaction in customer service can make all the difference. Organizations can achieve great design leaps in products but fail in how they provide service to customers. Remember Uber and the damage done to their brand because of how they are perceived to treat women? Innovation is about putting the user at the center of everything you do and empathically crafting the product, service, or way of operating.

Fail Ugly

The expression "If you are proud of your product, you are too late to market" hit me like a sledgehammer when I first heard it. Now there is a dilemma for all of us who were brought up hearing, "If a job is worth doing, it's worth doing well!" When do we put a new or amended product or service out in the market? Most of us would answer, "When it is finished!" Putting an unfinished product or service into the market goes against everything we have been taught. But OpenTable, the app for booking restaurants, prefers the expression "fail ugly." They want new products and ideas to fail ugly on launch so they can learn and rapidly iterate the idea. This mantra and way of operating would make most of us run a mile. And so it should—not away from it, but toward it!

As a business, we at Pi2 have learned how to reframe "80 percent failure" as success in order to build our resilience and innovation. We also have realized that the systems and habits of innovation and Design Thinking are the foundations of the Pi2 model. It is the key differentiator. With fresh ideas and thinking as wind in our sails, we are all set to create our "ding in the universe," as Steve Jobs put it. We have created the conditions to allow our followers to do the magic work they can do. This is the point at which you use that relationship credit with your followers to push them—to "professionally irritate" them—forward and to shape their own narratives.

Involving Your Team to Create Their Own Story: Creating the Playground

Leaders need to hold their team accountable for maintaining the "edge" they create. It's the position of not being comfortable, of being restless, dissatisfied, and driven to keep moving and stay ahead. To take a path less trodden and to take small risks requires conviction and a connection to your True North—and encouraging your people to take a course of action even when it may prove wrong. This phase draws heavily on the mandate, or trust bank, that you have built within your team. It will also test the systems and habits that you and your team have been building on your journey in order to make progress, learn from failures, and achieve successes toward your purpose.

So how do you develop your team into successful failers? Experimenters for themselves? All the supporting elements are in place, but how do you make them take the plunge? Once again, we return to the playground that is Design Thinking. We outlined the habits of Design Thinking in Chapter 2, and they are all integral to the playground. What is important here is that the leader keep things fresh so that small, incremental changes (in habits or the existing product set) are constantly being implemented. Failing early and fast becomes built into a culture of experimenting. The phases have a structure and, as on a playground, there are rules—but only to help the free flow of ideas and thinking that will speed early innovation. There are some conditions for success and some tools to help you on your way. They expand on what you already know.

Creative Spaces and Stimulants

Ideation is about creating blank spaces or canvases—whiteboards, blank walls, and empty spaces—to collaborate on and craft new ideas. Now, with collaboration apps like Miro and Sprintbase, this can be done virtually.

These innovation spaces need to be everywhere—ready at a moment's notice to pop up and be drawn on. Some companies create pop-up hubs in the space where they will be closest to the user or decision makers. Ideas are brainstormed, prototyped, and rapidly tested by living in them, showing them to the manufacturing side of the business, and rapidly putting them into production. The space that a leader creates in the playground for their team to experiment in is important.

The provision of the right stimuli includes the use of analogous situations. For example, a housing association looking to improve their repair services for their residents brought in a car breakdown service to talk to them. The association had a centralized repair center covering a wide range of property locations, and their response time to repair was poor. They wanted to learn from an analogous industry how to be better. They ended up creating mobile maintenance units that could locate themselves in the field and closer to the properties so they could more quickly respond to repair needs. You may also have heard of how IDEO brought in multiple versions of baby car seats to brainstorm ideas on how to create new shopping carts.

Innovation is a broad process that requires more than just Post-it Notes and cool offices. Observations and insights end up in an ideation process to be transitioned into new ideas. The following story of the bears and the power lines exemplifies ideation.

The Pacific Power and Light Company in Portland, Oregon, had a problem with ice forming on the power lines after snowstorms.

The ice had to be removed or over time the weight of it could break the electrical lines. The manual process of removing it was slow, tedious, and dangerous. So they gathered some brainstorming teams from different departments in the company: linesmen, managers, secretaries, and supervisors.

During a break, one of the linesmen shared with some of the participants how he had once come face-to-face with a big brown bear when he was servicing the power lines, and how he narrowly escaped being mauled by it. Upon returning to the meeting, someone else built on the linesman's story, suggesting training brown bears, which were very common in the area, to climb the poles and shake off the ice from the wires. No one laughed. Instead, they wondered how they could get the bears to climb and shake the poles. Hmmm ... why not put pots of honey at the top of the poles?

A brainstorm then began on how to get the pots of honey on the top of the poles. Someone threw out the idea of using helicopters to do the job. Silence ensued as people thought. Eventually, they turned back to how else to get the honey pots onto the poles. How much effort it would take to place pots of honey at the top of every electrical pole? Would it work?

And then the voice of a secretary, who had been sitting quietly in the meeting, broke through: "Won't the downwash from the helicopters break the ice and blow it off the wires?"

There was silence, and then the team started to realize that it could work. They tested the idea and it proved to be a good one. Today, all Pacific Power and Light has to do to remove ice from the wires is to charter a helicopter to fly at low altitude above the electrical wires and the downwash from the helicopter does all the work. Linesmen no longer have to risk their lives climbing the electrical poles.

So when we are in the ideation and creative space, remember the bears. No idea is stupid. It can lead to an answer.

In his book *Tools of Titans*, Tim Ferriss quotes Seth Godin: "People who have trouble coming up with good ideas, if they're telling you the truth, will tell you they don't have very many bad ideas. But people who have plenty of good ideas, if they're telling the truth, will say they have even more bad ideas. So the goal isn't to get good ideas; the goal is to get bad ideas. Because once you get enough bad ideas, then some good ones have to show up."

The rules of brainstorming are the lifeblood of IDEO. They see brainstorming as a core skill that has best practice ground rules and systems that encourage wild ideas. For example, they have a facilitator to help the groups do their best work. They also take great care in how they create their brainstorming areas. Just like a great chef, they prepare their environment for their creativity session. They put up pictures that quickly provide visual stimulus to the members of the brainstorming team. They shoot for quantity because they have proven that a focus on volume will produce quality. Inherent in that goal is the desire to keep the team from judging ideas as they go along. They make sure visuals are added to each Post-it Note to quickly hotwire the idea to the minds of others. Even the most basic of drawings conveys more than words.

Prototyping and Testing

Imagine that you are sitting in front of Disney's chief creative officer and you have just had devastating feedback about an early screening of your movie in which an ice queen is pitched against a young heroine. The movie is a dud and the storyline is tired and dated. Then imagine you're getting this feedback with eighteen months to go until the release date for the movie. Now imagine your leader encourages you to go and explore, and says, "You should take as long as you need to find the answers." As L. David Marquet describes it, the leader called, "Stop the play!" Now imagine that your team starts to question basic assumptions of the movie (which had been based on Hans Christian Andersen's "The Snow Queen") and the producer asks, "What could be right about the movie?" "If you could envisage anything on the screen, what would you want to see there?" The ideas started flowing. "What if the ice queen did not have to be a villain?" "What if the ice queen and the heroine are sisters?"

If you've seen the movie *Frozen*, you know what happened. The prototype that failed led to huge success with Olaf the Snowman,

Anna the heroine, and Elsa, her sister, the ice queen, who sings that catchy (but annoying) song, "Let It Go."

There are many other examples of the same process. The fact that Pixar screens early versions of their movies expecting them to fail ugly means that their people don't defend—they listen. Prototypes give the viewers, in this case, a sense of the idea, which allows them to provide a feedback loop that drives a better result. The cute kid in *Monsters, Inc.* was not a cute kid at first. Even simple testing of simple concepts that seem to be surefire winners reveals early feedback on ideas and can save large amounts of time and effort.

Prototyping can be very simple—as simple as a storyboard with four segments outlining how the user will interface with the idea, or as a prototype made with a few bits of office supplies. When IDEO was working with a company to design a surgical tool to operate on sensitive nasal tissues, they were having a hard time pinning down what the surgeon was trying to describe. An engineer ran off and grabbed a marker, an empty film canister, a clothespin, and some sticky tape, and in five minutes put together a prototype and showed it to the surgeon. The surgeon said, "Yes, something like this!" And with a few tweaks and designing it out, the prototype became a successful tool: the Diego Surgical System. And in this case the customer was involved.

Including Your Customer in Your Playground

The relationship with customers is part of a leader and team's mandate to innovate and create an edge. Remember my client Drew Cameron and his teachable point of view? "When things are going well, go and tell your client. When things are going badly, run and tell your client!" The principle is clear: share successes and failures with the customer. The result for Drew was that the client trusted him and his team so much that they came to new contract planning sessions with no legal representation. Decisions were made because the client was involved in the playground and trusted the experimentation and approach that Drew brought with his team. Now, *that* is trust in today's environment of legal cover and procurement.

Our work with one of our key clients, Akamai, has been based on a partnership approach to fail early, fail often, fail forward. It has led to some excellent shared successes and, more importantly, shared failures. My client contact was Maureen Finn, and together we were pushing the boundaries of trialing new products. The risks for both of us were high, and I was still holding that fear of failure in my heart somewhere. The delivery of a program in Japan still resonates. It was a high-risk program, combined with the fact that we were dealing with a culture of leadership in Japan that is very different to my own or Maureen's experience. And it was deemed a failure straight out of the blocks. It is difficult to see how we could have been more wrong.

In Japanese culture, how you deal with failure is massively different from the way we do it in the United Kingdom or United States. We could not just "fix it." We needed to travel a path of humility and rebuild face and trust. It was the biggest, most high-profile failure of our relationship, and it taught us so much as Maureen and our team started to learn how to work with their Asia team. We built a consensus-led design and delivery process that allowed us to buy our end client into the design process and outputs. It was innovative for its time in our work and is a process that we still use to this day.

Failures like that one have been painful, but because of the relationship, the learning is shared: there are equally high stakes for both parties; there is the potential win of learning how to deal with a key market or client; and the learning is based on an agreed way of approaching the challenge and the same measures. Always remember: your mandate as a leader includes your customers. The vision that we will both be celebrating new and innovative ways to develop leaders keeps us operating at a high level.

Leaders Should Be Close to Their End Customers

It's an oddity of the traditional organizational hierarchy that the customer is meant to come first and yet within the organization the leaders who make most of the decisions are the furthest from them. It usually falls to the bottom of the classic hierarchy pyramid—the call center operators, receptionists, cashiers, and waitstaff—to actually perform the interactions with customers on which the reputation and the value of the brand rest. As customers, we've all been in situations where interacting with another human who actively aims to improve the quality of our interaction has given us an added lift and a strongly positive brand experience. Yet all too often staff are not empowered to do this, and at worst this can even cause needless hassle for the customer and leave a sour taste.

I think of the day that my family and I checked into Claridge's in London. We were early and decided to head out for a walk, but we left our morning purchases at the front desk, which included dolls that my daughters had bought. When we returned to check in later, we were taken to our room. At the door, the lady checking us in turned to my young daughters and, putting a finger to her lips, said "Shhh!" in a soft tone. She opened the door quietly and crept in. The lights were low and the curtains shut. Their double bed was there and at the bottom of the bed, the Claridge's team had created a mini bed. The girls' dolls were tucked in "asleep." A look of wonder and amazement appeared on my daughters' faces. A moment of magic had been created.

How does a leader build and sustain that magic without being on the service end of their operations? The human-centric approach to Design Thinking means that a leader must place the customer at the heart of creating their edge. That means the leader and their team getting out from behind their desks and observing and exploring in the path of their customer. Being the CEO of the company, I am constantly advised to stop delivering for clients. My answer is always the same: the magic and learning happens in the workshops or the client conversations. The observations and raw feedback in the room can be difficult to hear, the insights are deep and rich—but I would not be exposed to both if I were not present. Data in this case for me becomes fresh and unfiltered. Time the leader spends serving customers or sorting out customer issues is time well spent. My colleague Simon Scott, while coaching and supporting the CEO, spent significant time in Marks & Spencer on the night shift stocking the shelves to learn how that shift affected the customer experience. The observations and insights led to store changes that benefited the customer.

All Prepared for Your Spontaneity Session

When the people at the front line of your organization are given a script to follow, it is intended to drive and ensure consistency across the board. In theory, there is much to be said for this—it gives the brand a strongly controlled voice and means that customers experience consistency. The trouble is that every human being is different and the context to every situation is different. The script needs to be about making the front-line team "all prepared for their spontaneity session." The team needs to experiment with different approaches and, through purposeful practice, develop an agile way to deliver to customers. Leaders need to provide a strong sense of direction and high freedom to act.

A script remains a script; a menu remains a menu. But even when an error is made, if the service is innovative, it can overcome that error. My favorite innovative failure of service came during that same stay at Claridge's. At dinner, the dessert orders were being taken and a new waiter asked my daughters what they wanted for dessert. My eldest daughter asked for ice cream and my youngest daughter asked for an apple. Seemingly simple requests. After twenty minutes—which is a long time for ice cream and an apple to be prepared—the waiter came back to apologize for the delay. He said that the kitchen was just finishing making the apple ice cream and it would be out soon.

Now, you might see that as poor listening and an error on the waiter's part. It was not what the girls had ordered. But out of that experience I had a real understanding of what it takes to run a luxury hotel and create "wow" moments for guests. It was also an eye-opener about what was possible. And guess what: I am writing about that story with a positive message, despite the error.

And yes, when you empower your front-line staff to experiment around protocol, you're potentially giving them free rein to cause a lot of damage. Even following the strictest set of rules, an employee working in the moment may not create a satisfactory experience for the customer. And even with the freedom to experiment, they may still fail. But when an employee spots an opportunity to go the extra mile, is presented with an unexpected customer issue, or simply spots a chance to iterate around how they usually behave, something wonderful can happen.

Can you empower all of your staff across your organization to react and experiment to make the most of each moment? If one staff member might offer a free perk or service that another would charge for, it could spell chaos for the integrity of the brand and customer trust. However, if your staff are engaged and aligned with your purpose, the risk of chaos is at least mitigated. Maintaining an edge is about taking risks, putting down the script, and seeing if your improvisation flies or fails.

Observing with Empathy

At one point, GE Healthcare Systems had a major issue: children were not reacting well to their CAT scanners. The noise of the scanners made the children so afraid, they had to be sedated to go through the process—which further increased their fear and risk. The designer of the CAT scanner was horrified when he saw a little girl crying on her way to the machine he had designed. He now had a new challenge: How might they create a scanner that children love? IDEO conducted fieldwork and identified a critical fact: the bedrooms of sick kids lacked some key things compared to those of healthy kids. There were no pictures of winning sports trophies or holidays—celebrations and tokens of enjoying life. The insight was that sick kids had the fun sucked out of their life! So how could they change that?

The ideation phase delivered the solution by modeling it on theme parks. The designers developed CAT scanner centers that mirrored a visit to a theme park with pirates and adventure. The scanners were decorated for the theme—for example, like a pirate ship. The kids had costumes. Getting a CAT scan was no longer just an appointment the children had to get through—it was now an experience they could participate in. Not surprisingly, patient satisfaction scores went up to 90 percent.

Again, in Design Thinking, the ability of the team to get out from behind their desks and observe the users in their environment is essential. It is also essential that a wide range of users, not just the average user, are observed. Observing and conducting fieldwork will include interviews with extreme users.

When conducting Design Thinking training, we have found that this is one of the most profound learning experiences for leaders and individuals. It is not about learning the questions, but rather the fact that they are not allowed to pass judgment on the information being provided. "What is your best experience of…?" and "What is your worst experience of…?" are followed not by judgments but by further questions digging deeper into the first response. No challenge or agreement is allowed, either. Just pure curiosity, consistently asking why. Each question that digs deeper into the answer and the real reasons for behavior or choices drives toward richer data and greater solutions. By the fifth "why" question, it is amazing the insights we are able to gain and the ideas that we generate.

Even so, as leaders in a position to go out and solve our customers' problems, sometimes we remain blind to the real problem.

My onetime neighbor Ms. Brown had a fuel consumption problem with her car. After the fifth time of taking it in to be checked without diagnosis, she was asked by a mechanic to "show him." So she took him out for a drive. She got in behind the wheel and pulled out the manual choke on the dashboard—which affects fuel usage—and hung her handbag on it. And so the problem was solved by "showing," and in the same way, an idea was formed for an additional feature for the car: a place to hang your handbag. The issue needed to be explored with curiosity to bring the "experiment" element to life and create new ideas.

So we as leaders are being thoroughly disruptive, creative, and innovative, and our teams are doing the same, and our customers are on board as well. But how do we know that we are still on course? Implied in the playground of "experiment" and explicit in some of my examples above is that we will get feedback and other information about how we are doing. Next, we'll look at where that might come from and how it can best be used.

So What? Experiment

Suggested System: Design House

As a business, we at Pi2 have crafted the concept of a system called Design House. The analogy of the system is that the house has many rooms. When we look at our products, we have many that are great and fit our purpose. But just as with any products, they may need a makeover. That's when they are checked into the Refresh Room of the Design House. Other times, somebody will identify a new product area, such as Conscious Decision Making (looking at how to manage bias in our decisions). That product is checked into the New Product Room, where it is readied for prototyping with a client. You get the picture. There is a room for archiving old products. There is a room for New Partner Products, where they are tested. That system is governed by our head of product, Ian Moore, and is reported on at our leadership team meetings. The system is structured to ensure it is fed and maintained in the right way.

Suggested Habits

1 Explore new products: One of my favorite habits is "squirrelling," or looking around for new ideas for products and approaches. At worst, it is annoying to my team, as I bring in new ideas that shake up their world—particularly for the consultants who deliver the new ideas. At best, it keeps our ideas fresh by having our radar in the market.

2 Prototype: Making it a habit to send in a half-finished product to your clients and test it live with them is something I never would have thought of before four years ago, when I was working with Maureen

Finn. Before that, we would have passed it as "finished" and then sold it. The benefits of early feedback and avoiding wasted time on perfecting a potentially flawed product are massive.

3   Get into the field: A key habit for me as a leader is to get out from behind my desk and spend time observing my team and customers. I will never stop producing content, just to be able to see how we can deliver on different and changing needs.

Disruptor: Challenge

I remember hosting an Investors Day with a client during which one of the groups pitched the courageous idea of investing in "loss leader" relationships with up-and-coming businesses that could not afford the services at the current time. The idea was a form of "pay it forward": giving something now to businesses to build social capital. The aim was that when they reached scale big enough for the bigger deals, the company was already engaged.

The idea was shot down. By the most senior person in the room. Not even an experiment or a prototype. Critical thinking had just killed off an idea because it did not fit our criteria. It was like a comedy program I watch: "Computer says no!" The looks on the faces of the group whose idea it was were interesting—anger and resilience. "This is the future!" said one of the team.

So who got this right and who got it wrong? The senior leader had not spent enough time looking through the "desirability" lens—considering what the customer wants. A fixed mindset based on how things already were had killed the idea. As a leader and design thinker, it is critical to keep yourself and your team looking through the lens of desirability for as long as possible. Quickly, then, you can move to prototyping and testing the idea. The other key thing that was missing before the idea was shot down: challenges around the original problem statement and the measures of success.

Having been brought up in an education system that values critical thinking often leads us to squash ideas. We need to challenge this tendency if we want to agitate for the future. There is a time for tough decisions, but it comes after the hard work of prototyping and testing. That is when the challenge can be brought forth and, if necessary, ideas can be killed off.

The tension between the "experiment" and "challenge" roles in the Disruptor style of leadership is vital to how leaders navigate their role. The fact that experimenting feels risky and goes against natural judgment for many leaders requires checks and balances. It requires systems and habits that allow leaders and their teams to release the natural critical thinking to cull those ten ideas or experiments down to two and to redeploy resources to other areas and ideas.

How Are We Doing? Leading Indicators

Imagine that the leader above had gone with a prototype of investing in one of their new clients. Imagine that investment is US$20 million into the business to use as capital to develop and shape the company. Now bring yourself to the point when you realize that the burn rate is going to be US$1 million a month. Would you not want to know that the business was heading in the right direction? Also, wouldn't it be great to know when you should stop the clock and call time on the idea? In lean start-up philosophy, Eric Ries describes the measures to do this. He calls them "leading indicators." They will tell you whether you are on the right track. But they are difficult to set, let alone measure or even trust. If only we had a crystal ball.

Leading indicators are the opposite of the lagging indicators that most organizations and individuals use now—the accounts for last year, average sales per head, your weight loss over time. At their simplest level, leading indicators are sign-ups to mailing lists or demonstrations of products, and the ongoing increase in sign-ups for your social media–based newsletter or offers. At their more complex level, for leaders measuring their personal resilience, they are the speed to recovery from stressful situations. In sport, athletes train to recover quicker from high-intensity moments. With Headspace, I train daily to allow my mind to self-correct more easily in periods of stress. The number of times I react badly in a stressful situation as a leader is a leading indicator of my underlying resilience.

The number of sick days that your team takes can be a leading indicator of an underlying problem with the team or culture. But sometimes those measures can lead you to a novel solution. I love the story of Asda, a UK supermarket chain, which had a chronic problem with absenteeism. They did the right thing and got curious rather than punitive. Was it a measure that something was wrong with engagement, or was it something else? The usual answer to this feedback would have been to clamp down on offenders. Or to blame leaders. Instead, the leaders used the leading indicator data to act innovatively. They asked more questions and found that one of the main causes was family illness or unexpected childcare. An indicator was telling them something valuable. The leadership response was to put a flexible shifts system in place that allowed employees to find someone to take their shift for them when they needed, thereby increasing employee trust and engagement. The supervisors might have hated the power being taken away from them, but the absenteeism problem was solved. In fact, the engagement levels went up. The employees were trusted and the employer was flexible. One of their key leading indicators—absenteeism—was now a source of an increase in another leading indicator—engagement.

The Lenses of Feasibility and Viability

Our natural reaction, as a result of our hardwiring and upbringing, is to logically or intuitively challenge an idea that is brought to us. We use our existing mental maps to critically analyze the idea. We're like the senior leader saying no to investing in smaller growth organizations: using old mental maps for making new decisions. In Design Thinking terms, we need to start with the lens of desirability and stay in that mode as long as possible, stretching our knowledge by observation and insight, to get a real understanding of what people's behavior shows us. Then we progress to the lenses of feasibility and viability.

This stage of critical thinking needs to be done with rigor and clear measures. You have set the leading indicators. You have a clear idea of what will tell you that the idea is on track. Now is the time for you as a leader to be ruthless and cull your ideas when they don't match your measures. Feasibility is whether we can actually do what is ideated—do we have the capability to deliver the product and service? Viability is whether it is commercially beneficial—will there be the right return on investment? The trick for the decision maker is to have a process that is not based on historical thinking or experience but rather focused on clearly defined leading indicators. The decision maker could be an individual leader or a group of advisors.

For our business, we have engaged an advisory board that is part of a system integral to our decision making. It comprises a group of people from multiple disciplines brought together to guide us in the tough decisions of when to double down on ideas and when to discard them. The fact that 20 percent success rates and 80 percent failure rates are celebrated in this space is crucial to helping us understand that our experimentation and Design Thinking will have a tough challenge coming when it faces our board. It is a tangible measurement of being more wrong.

The trick of the 80 percent failure rate is that the experiments and their failures are small and made on a regular basis. This ensures that the risk is low, and as long as there is a review and learning mechanism in place—the feedback loop—the idea is moved forward or out. An example from the world of luxury hotels is the introduction of a "water menu" to test whether people would value paying more for water from certain regions in the same way they do for wine. The experiment did not last long—the feedback loop was flooded (so to speak) with the environmental cost of shipping and bottling water, and the idea sank.

Maintaining an Edge

Building systems and habits based in Design Thinking with clear leading indicators so you can make quick decisions results in a thriving system that allows you to keep a sustainable edge. The rise of data analytics within this idea is no coincidence. Your decisions need to be fed by the monitoring and well-informed use of the data mined from leading indicators. In "challenge" mode, the leader is willing to challenge in a robust way with refreshingly direct conversations, and their success comes from how they set up capturing and monitoring the right data. The key word here is "right." The leader should also encourage the team to challenge their own ideas in the same way.

In *Black Box Thinking*, Matthew Syed comments that in testing, it's often only the successes that are captured and monitored. The problem with this is that information gets missed when you don't analyze the failures. As a stark illustration of this, he gives the example of aviation, where so many major innovations have arisen from deaths—the cause of which must surely be the most extreme form of failure. It's bold, but it clearly makes the point that it's not until you stress-test your ideas that you discover the weak points.

This also highlights how innovations can be driven by crises in particular. It has to be a paradox that most people and organizations don't court crises, yet the results of crises give the richest feedback for change. When something has to change, it always does. If left alone, that change could come merely in the form of a gradual decline. These are the moments that need a shot of crisis, and that can be hard to engineer. Special forces and emergency services know this all too well. These organizations use their downtime to train and stretch their capabilities. Whether it is training in arctic conditions, under live fire, or in a disorientating smoke-filled simulator, they are courting failure in order to capture the data that will generate innovation in decision making and ways of working. Research on legendary firefighters, renowned for knowing when to pull their teams out of fires before a building collapsed, unsurprisingly found that they had a heightened sense of observation, and therefore insight, from years of purposeful practice in simulations and real experience in fires.

This is why having an edge is about keeping your team on their toes. They've got to be constantly looking for what could be better. The energy needs to be up and the excitement palpable. This is where the relationship credit you've built up with your team gets spent: keeping them at the edge of their comfort zone, always striving for better and straining to learn more. You give praise when things go right. You feel pleasure when they themselves say that things could still be improved.

Constantly seeking an edge and being restlessly dissatisfied can be draining. It can take teams to their stress threshold. But, as I've been saying all along, with the right people, the right systems, and the right habits, it can be the greatest place to live and work. As a leader, though, you need to first show up and prove that you can live there yourself. We've covered the resilience you need to maintain that effort and approach. You have created systems and habits that fuel the energy in others and therefore the innovation. The role of challenger is about setting these up to work.

The truth is, the word "innovation" is the glossy term for "a lot of hard work." As we have seen in the "experiment" role, the hardest part of innovating is failing. So the systems, habits, and purposeful practice we need in order to embed a culture of failure require an infinite mindset, not a finite mindset, as Simon Sinek says in *The Infinite Game*. This is a life's work for the leader.

Making It Safe to Fail, Reflect, and Learn

It doesn't matter how innovative you want to be. When it's not safe to be wrong, people avoid it. Would you test out your tablecloth-pulling skills the first time you meet your partner's family? Would you jump off a cliff without knowing how deep the water below was? How about ordering orange juices when it's your round at the pub?

In most non-life-threatening situations, you need other people to make it physically and psychologically safe for you to fail. Of course, this is by necessity the basis of a risk-taking culture. When leaders make it safe, and even positive, to derive insights from being wrong, the possibilities immediately start fanning out.

In your role as Host, you have already encouraged your team to form its own habits and systems for sharing those insights, and in doing so, you have made each team member responsible for their own work while benefiting from membership in the supportive group. An important feature of this is the creation of active and immediate feedback loops that provide a free flow of information on which decisions throughout your team can be made, without necessarily being escalated to you. And it will be clear which decisions should be escalated to you.

That feedback loop is internal to your organization. Being restless and dissatisfied, however, means that you will be thirsty for information from other sources.

A colleague of mine had an expression that he used as a presupposition in his development. Like most people, he suffered from not liking to hear feedback on himself. It always surprised me, as I thought he was very good at putting the feedback process in place and receiving it. It was only when we started to do presupposition work as part of personal effectiveness that he told his audience and us that he held a mantra in his head: "My critics help me!" It allowed him to hear and see the feedback as an opportunity to grow and be more open to and curious about gathering more feedback. As he became more used to working in this way, he was able to embed the positive impact of that open feedback loop.

The Advisory Board, the Growth Board, and the Customer Board

I have mentioned our advisory board: three people whose role it is to advise me and my COO on our journey as a business. Advisory boards can take many shapes. In our case, the board's focus is "noses in, fingers out": they ask questions, pay attention to what's happening, and give insight, but they don't directly involve themselves in running the business. Members meet with us three times a year and have access all year round to us and our business. These meeting days have been the toughest in my career—I'm popping headache pills by lunchtime. Why? Because they ask critical questions and provide differing points of view that cause us to question our approach in a 360-degree way. They challenge us about focus—too wide? too narrow? (the latter has never been a problem for me). They challenge us about basic things like culture or people's roles.

They are—in the nicest possible way—professional irritants. They provide valuable irritation to ensure our focus is just right. They come from different backgrounds as well. So their challenges are diverse on many topics, including finance, marketing, sales, and people. Being external to the business, they provide a valued source of data and feedback.

We could have had a growth board as well. The concept of growth boards in start-up businesses is about bringing together a group of people with mixed functional expertise and accountabilities and using real live data and data analytics to make robust decisions about where to lay the bets for new products, ideas, and approaches.

The statistics that L. David Marquet lays out in his book *Leadership Is Language* show that a large percentage of the worst decisions are made when the leader does not listen to their team. Surely, one might think, this would be the opposite in that they are the most experienced? But no. The point is that for a leader, experience and ego can be helpful or they can be a problem. As I've said several times before, as leaders, we need to engage the collective wisdom of our teams and the people around us to improve our decision making. This concept is highlighted in the challenge of Design Thinking and innovation. The growth board ensures that decisions are made after all voices have been heard and all points of view have been explored. They bring a rigorous process to play with clear measures. Leave your ego and a lot of your expertise at the door. Bring in others' observations and ideas—it makes for better decisions.

We are also looking at forming a customer board. This is a group of customers—from our fans to our detractors—who will be refreshingly direct with us on how we are doing and the direction we are taking.

The customer board is not a focus group. In Design Thinking, focus groups are not valuable. Remember what Henry Ford supposedly said: "If I had asked my customers what they wanted, they would have said faster horses." When Steve Jobs launched the iPod, it was not a raging success, but he did not mind. His vision went beyond that to iTunes and online music storage—something that at the time was not on any customer's mind.

So what is the customer board, exactly? For us, it will be a group of customers who understand our journey and know where we are going. They will be up to speed on our purpose and our history. From this, they will be able to quickly bring thoughts and critical feedback to bear on our evolving products and service. They will also allow us to peek around the corner with them on their journey and see how we can adapt to help them.

Whether it is by establishing a board or not, it is critical to keep customers in your feedback loop. If you are already partnering with them for innovation, their involvement in the feedback loop is probably already happening. But if you are not in that situation already, it can be tricky to engineer. For example, how many of us have had a quiet dinner interrupted at a restaurant, maybe more than once, by the question from the server, "How is everything with your food?" The trick is creating feedback loops that feed innovation that might actually delight rather than annoy our customers.

Creating Feedback Loops with Your Customers

You know you are going in the right direction, and you are now on the journey to achieve your quest. Yet there are times in your journey where you find yourself almost back to where you started despite hard work and good ideas. There have been many times in our business when my COO and I have observed that we are back in the same old loop, like Sam and Frodo who on the way to Mordor, in the cold and driving rain, find themselves having gone in circles. The kind of loops we need are feedback loops in all our endeavors and systems to tell us how we stand, so that even when we end up in the same place, we at least now know a route that does not work.

So how do you create feedback loops with your clients or users? In innovation terms, organizations are on a spectrum of innovation maturity: from the basic level of buying into Design Thinking through to training their people; from embedding Design Thinking into everything the organization does through to the ultimate level, where innovation and Design Thinking are done in deep partnership with users and clients. It's the same for a head of internal audit partnering closely with the regulator in financial services to innovate ways to increase assurance for shareholders, investors, and customers as it is for Procter & Gamble innovating live with their customers. The ultimate goal is to have innovation and Design Thinking embedded in all employees, in all teams, and in all interactions with clients. Openly talking about and practicing Design Thinking and learning fast with our clients causes them to want to be involved, and we are able to involve them in a fast response feedback loop. This symbiotically requires and creates a deeper partnership and building of trust.

So I think you get the picture by now. There is no such thing as too much feedback from different sources in your role as Disruptor. This combination of feedback from the boards, from the data produced against leading indicators, and from your followers is critical to progress. Reliable, immediate data and information are critical to the everyday conversations you will have with your team, and it supports you in the deeper conversations you will have in your role as Catalyst.

So What? Challenge

Suggested System: Advisory Board

As a leader, you need to hold yourself accountable for progress against key leading indicators in the business, but you'll also need help. In this respect, you'll find it useful to set up your own advisory board. We pay our advisory board for their time, but in our toughest times during the COVID-19 pandemic, they worked for free. You could set up advisory boards from within your network by using the "pay it forward" approach. Acting as each other's advisory board is a beneficial setup. You need to pick people whose attitude, skill set, and experience have added huge value to you in achieving your purpose. Then formalize their role. Remember: noses in, fingers out.

Suggested Habits

1 Shoot for an 80 percent failure rate: Adopt the habit of seeing 80 percent failure as a success. If you are not achieving that in the many low-cost, low-risk experiments you make, you are not stretching yourself enough.

2 Do a premortem: Make a habit of peeking around the corner to see whatever disasters might befall you. It allows you to be clear on the leading indicators you can use to measure success and the degree of challenge needed. Imagine that a project has failed massively and then work back to suggest what could have happened.

3 Create feedback loops with clients: The habit of creating feedback loops against agreed areas of performance and expectation at the beginning of projects sets you and your clients up to measure and challenge progress effectively.

10

catalyst

TALI SHAROT FINALLY gave up. She decided to leave graduate school at Harvard and return to New York. And that's when it happened.

In her podcast about our power to change others, Sharot talks about her toughest time: her very bright supervisor at Harvard would not allow her to settle for lesser projects or research topics. She spent a year being rejected by the supervisor, to the point that she decided to quit and go back to New York. It was only when she gave up, fell out of her current thinking, and relaxed that she suddenly had a revelation and chose the topic that has inspired her to this day. Her revelation was that her knowledge of optimism and neuroscience was not enough to give her an answer to her True North—her purpose—and her work now integrates neuroscience, behavioral economics, and psychology to study how emotion influences people's beliefs, decisions, and social interactions. Her supervisor challenging her and encouraging her not to take an easy path—which she says she would otherwise have taken—was instrumental in her success. It took a Catalyst, acting as a coach and mentor—and a stubborn one at that—to nudge Sharot in the right direction, and then falling out of her own thinking to bring inspired action.

The roles of mentor and coach are often not independent and both are required. But each plays a distinct and different part. As a leader, you need to be agile in both roles.

Let's return to our playground for a moment. As kids, we know the playground is a relatively safe psychological space and that it gives us the freedom to develop our own sets of rules: groups form and we are instinctively part of them or we are not. We have an inbuilt instinct to choose those groups that suit us best, and while we may be attracted to and want to be part of other groups, if we don't have the "skills" or in other ways enhance the group, it is made clear to us, with childlike ruthlessness, that we don't fit.

But the playground is always supervised, and we can ask for help by speaking to a supervisor, saying that we are being excluded from a particular group. The supervisor can then show or tell us what we need to do to be part of that group, or guide us toward starting a group of our own. The supervisor is effectively mentoring and coaching us. In addition, if we feel ill at ease within a group, we can benefit from the experience of our peers within that group to help us integrate. We wouldn't use the word, but they are, in their own way, acting as our Catalyst.

As a leader, you have a responsibility to maintain your mandate to lead through being a Catalyst, to develop the capability of your followers. In the Pi2 model, the Catalyst recognizes the fact that at some point there is a need to stop, pause, and reflect with your team members before engaging with life and challenges again. This is done through teaching robust, well-tested points of view and enabling their own self-reflection and growth mindset. This style is both reflective and developmental in nature and embodies the dual skills of being a mentor and a coach.

Mentoring, in my experience, involves taking a stance with a point of view, or series of points of view, from which others can benefit. These are teachable points of view. You are building capability in others through sharing your own insights, perspectives, and experience. Mentoring is integral to my business's advisory board and has a place at varying stages in the journey we are undertaking. The advisors on that board have been a revelation in their impact on our direction and success. Mentoring is modeling.

The benefits of reverse mentoring are equally important. This is when you engage the more junior members of your team and organization to benefit from the collective wisdom and points of view of your wider team.

Coaching is building capability in others by unlocking their personal potential through questioning, prompting self-reflection, and reframing. It demonstrates the value of silence, questioning, and skilled and appropriate feedback. It is underpinned by the art of curiosity. Coaching is questioning without a solution or a point of view in mind. Try beginning with, "What's on your mind?"

There are various accrediting bodies (e.g., the International Coaching Federation) throughout the world working to establish professional benchmarks for coaches and mentors, and the sheer number of bodies alone makes it difficult for me as a practitioner to endorse any particular one. This has created tension and a challenge for me, primarily in the coach's role of giving advice. If I were accredited as a coach, I would struggle to call my sessions "coaching" sessions mainly because the more sophisticated conversation requires a balance of coaching and mentoring. My experience, together with feedback from my coachees, indicates that the label is not helpful. What is helpful is being able to adjust the conversation in the moment to the needs of the person in front of you.

Don't get me wrong. One of my favorite books, *The Coaching Habit*, written by one of my favorite people, Michael Bungay Stanier, is spot on in that we need to keep our "advice monster" under control and be a bit more coachlike in our approach as a leader. There needs to be a way of smoothly creating a more sophisticated conversation. This would allow the Catalyst to move spontaneously and appropriately from being a coach, believing the answers and wisdom lie in the person in front of them, to being a mentor and sharing advice. That is a conversation style most of the leaders I work with can buy into. And I have tried to demonstrate it in the examples I give for both mentor and coach.

As for all of the leadership styles, a refreshingly direct mindset is important. However, that mindset is particularly vital for the success of both the mentor and coach. Equally vital for the Catalyst are the principles of psychological safety. These roles demand that the leader ask for and encourage interpersonal risk-taking, and there is an embedded obligation of candor in the way this is delivered.

Catalyst: Mentor

The guide archetype is crucial in the hero's journey—think Gandalf, Dumbledore, Mary Poppins. The ability to shape lives and provide ideas for the direction in others' lives while still leaving them to make their own decisions is a very strong skill.

My former boss Ian Ritchie was a classic example of the guide. He had an amazing ability to make you feel in control of your decisions but also that he had a hand close to the tiller if you needed it. There was never a doubt that he would back my decisions, even the basic decision on a company car. I wanted a car that was assigned to people above my level and I thought I would push my luck and ask. He crafted a conversation that I will always remember. I had the right to ask, but I also had responsibilities for that choice. He simply said, "What's in it for me if I say yes?" I replied, "More sales!" Deal.

Ian was guiding me to understand that choices come with responsibilities. He taught me how to make people feel free to make choices, but also to guide them to understand the cost of those choices, to stretch themselves, and to deliver on promises. So many people feel the world owes them a living or that if you ask, then you will get. It is a journey on which parents try to take their children, teaching them the value of things as they grow up. This does not end when they become leaders. Guiding is still needed. As a Catalyst a leader is about stretching their followers while guiding them on their choices and accountabilities.

Teachable Points of View

The concept of teachable points of view (TPOV) has been part of leadership storytelling for a while. Mentoring is not, as one of my colleagues would say, "pin your ears back and listen to me telling you how good I am." It is taking a point of view on how things should be done and crafting it into a proven hypothesis from which others can benefit.

I can think of some outstanding examples of TPOV: Drew Cameron's "When things are going well, go and tell your client. When things are going badly, run and tell your client!" Ian Ritchie's "If you go spend time with your clients, you will get business!" Another point of view Ian had was, "Profit is freedom!"—that is, give me more sales and you have the choice to have a better company car. Susan Cain, the bestselling author of *Quiet: The Power of Introverts in a World That Can't Stop Talking*, has a TPOV that writers will be successful only if they "take survival off the table"—in other words, having other jobs takes the pressure off their creative art. My former HR director Jim Snowdon always told me to pay more than the candidate expected so that when they joined the organization, they felt valued and money was off the table as an issue for them.

The TPOV are usually easy to grasp. Andrew Webster, my guru, constant mentor on this journey, and member of my advisory board, supports the TPOV that I should run my business as a series, or stream, of small experiments. Of course I get the concept of the small experiments and how they release invaluable learning. But I struggle with it being constant and therefore keeping it front of mind. Andrew is the voice on my shoulder that keeps me true.

So what or who is your voice on your shoulder? What are the TPOV that keep you steady on course to your purpose? How clear are you on the key things you stand for as a leader and server of your followers and customers?

What Makes a Good Mentor?

Mentors can use leading indicators against which to measure themselves. When we train mentors, we use David Maister, Charles Green, and Robert Galford's work on the Trusted Advisor. For the Host: connect style, I gave the equation they use to measure trust:

$$\text{Trust} = \frac{\text{Credibility} + \text{Reliability} + \text{Intimacy}}{\text{Self-Orientation}}$$

The authors describe credibility as including the "in the room" and "CV" criteria that give an individual credibility, or not, in the eyes of another. Their "CV" is their track record, whether it is of delivering on projects, developing talent, or being a safe pair of hands through difficult times. In the past it was—and to a certain extent in certain businesses it remains—the school the individual went to. In themselves, however, these criteria are not enough to determine whether you are a good or bad leader and mentor, so the authors include "in the room" criteria. This is where your purpose, your identity, and your presence all have vital roles to play. When combined with your ability to be present, engaged, authentic, and refreshingly direct, your credibility in the eyes of your followers and clients becomes tangibly stronger.

The reliability element of the Trust Equation is as simple as "delivering on your promises." The ability to make judgments on expectations and deliver on them cannot be underestimated. "Being good at what you do" is the entry level for trust. Leaders should not be full of hot air. They should have a track record, created through their experiences of delivering on their promises. These don't stop when you get the leader badge and name. The promises become even more demanding.

The role Maister and colleagues give to intimacy might at first raise an eyebrow. However, if the sharp edge of leadership is based on authenticity, then at the heart of that is the ability to build deep relationships through intimacy. Don't mistake this for the ability to be liked. In their research on the difference between good advisors and outstanding advisors, the authors landed on the fact that outstanding advisor or guide relationships were built on respect rather than on being liked. The fact that you don't need to be friends with your advisors does not stop you from knowing that they are the first person you call when you want the honest, no-holds-barred version of the truth. In many cases, that intimacy also bridges cultural boundaries. The different needs and pace of the culture in China or the Middle East still require the same qualities in their advisors' attitude and skill set.

Intimacy is also necessary to allow the advisor to admit that their role has run its course or when they can't help—and also when a competitor might have the answers. "I am not right for you—but I know somebody who is" is a regular answer from an outstanding advisor. That requires the mentor and trusted advisor to maintain a healthy network to support their work.

In Maister, Green, and Galford's equation, the trust that is formed by your credibility, reliability, and intimacy can be diminished by what they call self-orientation. If you think about any relationship, it has a purpose, and with it, a degree of bias or self-interest. I run a consultancy business, and therefore part of my role is to drum up more business. This means that whether I like it or not, my clients will take some of my actions as a sales push. The perceived self-interest of a leader and a mentor can never be taken out of the equation, and it is important to acknowledge it. That simple acknowledgment alone goes a long way in lessening the impact of self-interest. However, there are other ways to diminish that impact and increase your trust.

Reverse Mentoring

One of the best ways to increase trust is to value the reverse impact of the mentoring relationship. Jose-Luis Guerrero, whom I met in HSBC, was an incredible leader who opened the sessions for the mentor-mentee training I ran. He told a powerful story of how mentoring had made an impact on him personally, and about the lessons he took from the people he mentored in his career. He started any mentor relationship with a two-way measurement of impact and value, where each conversation ended with statements about enjoyment and impact. This helped the mentee feel they were giving back and not wasting the time of a very important person. Cleverly and authentically, this amazing leader had crystallized a TPOV on mentoring that could be shared and acted on by his mentees. Many years later, I was teaching mentoring in a completely different organization and talked about him without naming him. One of the people in the room approached me afterward to check that the person I meant was the same one she had experienced in her past in an organization where he was, and it was. She was in a company with 250,000 people in it. It proved the lasting impact of the leader on creating a strong, open mentoring culture.

Another form of reverse mentoring is when senior leaders take on a mentor who is a junior in the company, or younger. Typically, the younger person gives the senior leader insight into what it is like to be led by them and their peers at the lower levels of the company. For many leaders, this also provides a view into the reality of relationships with key customers.

The other type of role in reverse mentoring is that of a muse. A senior (and older) leader in the apparel industry built a relationship with a person who represented the company's target market (young and liked the nightclub scene) to understand how decisions on their products were perceived by the end customer. This wider view of the team, which can include customers, end users, and other teams in the same organization, has a profound impact on the effectiveness of the leader as mentor. It also powerfully—through the point of view that customers and end users are at the heart of what you do—focuses the mind of the team on the fact that users need to be brought to the center of decision making across the organization.

Curiosity Is a Secret Ingredient

I cannot emphasize enough the value of curiosity in the leadership role. For the Catalyst especially, it is important to lead with curiosity first. As one of my colleagues, Alex Villar Hauser, taught me, if we don't lead with curiosity and build rapport and intimacy, then we'd better have masses of arrows to fire, as potential questions or points of view, at our followers to build their capability. By being curious, we can build a picture of the mindset, capability, confidence, and aspirations of the person in front of us. We can also start to help them focus by firing the killer arrow (question or point of view) that makes the biggest difference to them. When a coach or mentor asks the question, "What is the real issue here?" it is to put the bull's-eye on the nub of the challenge.

Curiosity comes in many shapes and forms. It can be in the mind of the mentor or coach. It can be in the form of observations of the individual in front of them. A coachee or mentee may be giving mixed messages: they say they are happy, but everything about their demeanor screams otherwise. Curiosity is that step forward as a coach or mentor to check out what they are observing—it can be as simple as, "You don't seem happy," or it can be a more subtle and riskier challenge about a range of observations. Your curiosity can help them realize that they're going through the motions or trying to fool people and it is not working. In more subtle ways, it can uncork a real explosion of self-awareness in the follower.

I significantly changed how I do things when Jacqueline Farrington challenged me with her curiosity about why I do what I do. Over a glass of wine, she pushed that curiosity to "professional irritant" level. I thought, *My purpose is to create heroes of the people I work with,* but it felt cheesy to me. It was only through her robust curiosity that the new purpose of our business was born.

Can a Line Manager Be Your Mentor?

When we at Pi2 engage with organizations to train their leaders as mentors, one of the key things we do is separate the role of a mentor from that of a line manager. Inevitably, one of the first questions to come up is whether individuals need a mentor if they have an outstanding line manager. Mentors have either a general counsel role or specific functional roles they play. As an example, take our advisory board. We have a digital products and innovation expert as mentor. We have an ex-managing director of Accenture as a business development expert. And we have a CFO of a midlevel bank as an advisor on commercials and investment. Each adds value on our voyage of discovery, bringing advice from a wider spectrum than just their focused experience.

With a line manager playing a mentor role, there is an inherent conflict of interest. As a follower or direct report, your pay and reward is at risk and your performance review is an obligation. And the role of the line manager in performance and alignment is sometimes clouded. When you are too close to the deliverables, it can be hard to give clarity to an individual. Having a second opinion on the alignment and performance is a good supporting benefit of a mentor. This means that although your line manager can be your mentor, it is always best to have other sources of mentoring.

So What? Mentor

Suggested System: Defined Points of View Based on Pain Points

Part of my struggle to believe that I am a credible person as a leader comes from all of the pain points that I have struggled with in my career: being overlooked for a promotion in The Oxford Group for valid reasons; basically being fired, or forced out, from Procter & Gamble for allowing a partner in my life to cause an error of judgment in how I used my company car—a long story and full of my inability at the time to have difficult conversations with my partner about how I managed my life and how they impacted it. Now I can have points of view that stop that same issue happening again for others. We all have pain points and lessons that are useful to other people to hear and learn from. What is the "T-shirt" you have because you have been there, done that? What is your secret sauce that you can pass on to other people in mentoring them? That system is the focus of your efforts. Your challenges and screwups, your being more wrong, adds value to others.

Suggested Habits

1   Your screwups are gold dust: Develop the habit of seeing screwups and mistakes as learning opportunities for you and your credibility as a mentor. Reviewing them and crafting them into TPOV promotes your value.

2   Be intensely curious: Seek first to understand before firing your arrows. Ensure that you have clarity as a mentor before tailoring your TPOV to the mentee.

3 Value being a mentor: Find, state, and reinforce the value you receive as a guide and a mentor. Make the person feel that they add value by asking you to guide them.

Catalyst: Coach

If you want a book on coaching in leadership, you can find one—in fact, you can find many, some of them excellent. The subject has been well covered, and in some ways done to death. And yet we seem to keep needing more. Why hasn't all this insight and teaching had the desired impact?

The answer is that coaching is perceived as something that takes a lot of time and effort. Most people think of it as like going for a ninety-minute gym workout when they know they have only twenty minutes or less. It needn't be so. That is the power of Michael Bungay Stanier's book *The Coaching Habit*. MBS (as he calls himself now to shorten the time people take to say it—see a theme?) had me at the tagline, "How to coach in 10 minutes or less." He also had me when he said all he was asking me to do was "be a bit more coach-like." Sure, I can do that.

So, with MBS's book as my starting point, let me outline my views on some of the key things I think coaching delivers in the context of the coach and mentor roles of the Catalyst.

Clarity

In an ideal situation, your team would be operating at the highest level of their performance and purpose. A person who's performing strongly but with a low sense of purpose is likely to be in what Jamie Smart calls "driven achiever" mode, which, as we've seen, is exhausting and ultimately counterproductive. An employee who's demonstrating low performance and low purpose may well be in the wrong role—or stuck.

As mentioned above, one of the leader's roles as mentor is to check for alignment of purpose and performance. The leader's role as coach is to dig deeper and check that the individual is certain of their own value, confidence, and conviction of the path they are on. This means that coaching can be about purpose, performance, or potential. The fact that most leaders focus their coaching on performance causes many people to see it as performance management, but, if the alignment and leading indicators are understood and cascaded, the simple truth is that coaching should be about development and purpose. And the role of coach is to help the individual dig down within themselves to find their own answers and insights.

When a person is working their socks off without being clear on why, the first thing I tend to do as coach is give them a needed pause in their pace. The coach's role at this point is the daunting one of convincing them—in the context of purpose—to go down to a feeling of low performance. Remember what is often said: the first sign of madness is doing the same thing and expecting different results. The coachee has to have a clear and stated purpose before they pick up the pace again, and it's the leader's work in coaching that will help them find it.

Get Others to Say for Themselves When They're Wrong

Encouraging others to go forth and be more wrong is intrinsically linked to getting them to return with fresh findings that can be transformed into insights—and specifically those that will help guide the team toward realizing their shared purpose. This is where the value of coaching emerges for the individual, the team, and ultimately the organization.

Coaching is a specific skill, and one that comes more naturally to some than others. My own tendency is to drive people forward and pump energy into the relationship with stories, role-modeling, and personal energy. So I find stepping back and leading with open questions more testing—it's a muscle I need to work harder to exercise.

The impact of the coachee finding their own answers fuels my change in approach to being "more coachlike." The coachee's role should not be about defending their actions. It's about them considering, analyzing, and drawing insights themselves. The coach's role is to question deeper to help and encourage this process. Part of that is you as a leader feeling comfortable enough to be wrong and readily share your failures and, importantly, the learning you have distilled from those failures.

A Powerful Moment—Coach or Mentor?

Not too long ago, my eldest daughter gave me a simple, powerful, devastating bit of feedback. I was trying to deal with a situation, pushing ahead and sure that I was handling it the right way, when she quietly kicked me under the table and whispered, "Bully."

I paused, stopped what I was doing, and had a deep moment that lasted at least four hours. She was so right and I had been so wrong, regardless of my intentions. Later, at home, as she was heading to bed, I sat her down and said simply, "Thank you!" We both had a tear in our eye as she walked away after a long hug.

She had been my coach that day—or had she been my mentor? She saw my behavior from a different position, called it as she saw it, and allowed me to reflect on it. You could say it was coaching, as she held up a mirror and let me come to my own conclusions. Or you could say it was mentoring, as she pulled on her experience of being at school and seeing that verbal behavior have an impact on her and her friends. Either way, it was her TPOV. She was being a Catalyst to change my mindset—and my behavior.

There are times when people don't realize they're wrong and need to be coached or mentored to look at the situation from a new angle so they can change. The coach's strength is not in having power over others; it's in holding up a mirror so that the coachee gains the data, and the power, to come to their own decisions and conclusions.

In the chapter on refreshingly direct conversations, I looked at the types of conversations this mindset fosters or all the leadership styles. There are, however, some refreshingly direct points that should be made with particular reference to the Catalyst role.

Professional Irritant

The Catalyst reinforces relationships, but only when kept in balance with connecting and engaging. Even in the moment of challenging or guiding another person, the sense of connection needs to feel strong, but this is naturally worn down through pushing. It's worth remembering, therefore, that operating in Catalyst mode is about highlighting the rights as well as the wrongs. It is a valuable time for highlighting the positives, praising, and flagging areas to work on. But don't look at this as wrapping your other comments in cotton wool: everything said in this sophisticated conversation has to be authentic and meaningful. It has to be honest and direct. It's about being a professional irritant.

The worst way to start a sentence as a Catalyst (and in most situations, in fact) is, "This might offend you, but . . ." It's easy to tell yourself that you're acknowledging the feelings of the person you're talking to when you say this, but in practice, the opposite is true. Each time you want to start a sentence this way, consider: What is your purpose in telling this person this thing in this way? If you know the answer, then you don't need the caveat. If you don't, then you're not speaking with purpose.

My former colleague Mike Taylor had a great way of addressing this. He used to say that the mind does not do negatives. If we say, "Don't think about oranges!" we will realize that the mind needs to think about oranges before it can not think about them. In the same way, starting conversations or parts of conversations with, "Don't take this the wrong way" or "The last thing I want to do is cause offense!" has the opposite effect of the one you desire. Being refreshingly direct should help you avoid prefacing difficult conversations this way. It is a clear model of feedback based on evidence, your curiosity about that person's 50 percent of the truth, and your desire to help them grow.

Developing the habits of regularly being a Catalyst also means that you get more practice at it and will find it easier to turn to during the stressful times when alignment and potential are stretched most taut.

Recognizing Value

Being a Catalyst to work on promoting the potential of a team member is essentially about recognizing the value in that person and investing in them. The role is based on asking open-ended, explorative questions and encouraging your people to provide their own ideas and test them out in a safe environment.

Being curious allows your coachees to explore the possible outcomes of their proposed actions. Your questions can then be about what experiments they can create to test their ideas. There need to be measures or leading indicators in place before they run the experiment and derive results from it. Following your curiosity as the Catalyst, your next question is therefore about the leading indicators they could have to show that their action is either moving toward their purpose or not. These questions are typically rigorous and tough, but they are designed to set up the team for powerful and valuable experiments.

Saying, "I don't think this is working, let's try something else" is particularly powerful because it's assertive and open as well as inclusive. It invites response, but it doesn't shy away from a clear-sighted view. Similarly, questions beginning with "How might we...?" are great for encouraging experimentation. They immediately make the coachee feel that their views and opinions are valued. They also implicitly recognize the alignment of your purposes. This is a way of engaging with someone through the challenge, not in spite of it, and it actively encourages divergent thinking. In turn, the ideas that emerge can be worked on and prototyped until the ideas converge on a solution. Crucially, it's asking the open questions, using divergent thinking, that provides scope for testing, being wrong, and personal discovery and growth.

Of all the leadership styles, I find the Catalyst the hardest. I tend toward energizing teams and painting pictures of the future because I have a strong point of view. But I've found that practicing asking more questions, without an agenda, with my team has been highly useful in helping me step back from the detail of the business and getting more comfortable with empowering others to adopt those roles.

What Do You Think of Me?

I mentioned earlier that one of my favorite questions with which to open a workshop session on leadership and personal effectiveness is, "What do you think of me?"

The "What Do You Think of Me?" exercise is about speaking directly and honestly. It is very powerful, so when used merely as a tool of vanity, it can be incredibly destructive. Empowering others to provide feedback in a way that lets their defenses down can be highly enlightening for both parties. It also provides the opportunity to demonstrate how to take feedback, be challenged, and recognize failure.

The next stage in the exercise is turning the tables and asking, "What do I think of you?" It's a charged moment that really sets people on edge, because it seems to anticipate something negative, or at any rate a statement from which they may need to protect themselves. Almost everyone finds it easier to give comment than to receive it, yet the value of feedback really resides with the receiver. It takes a lot of trust to get to this point, but it is an important opportunity to give the subject of the feedback valuable information that may even conflict with negative things they say about themselves. Most people are their own harshest critics, and when they can trust someone else to give them an alternative perspective, it can be very empowering.

When you recognize that everyone does form perceptions of everyone else, and those perceptions color their interactions, then logically, being able to discuss and challenge those perceptions can either reinforce them or sweep them away. And when you can be direct and honest with each other about such personal things, then discussing being wrong with each other should be no problem.

Role-modeling giving feedback is equaled in value only by demonstrating how to receive it, and then doing something about it. The culture of openness to feedback should spread through the team, so that everyone supports each other in testing, pushing the boundaries, and talking about being wrong—and then doing something about it.

No Stigma to Being Wrong

In a book celebrating the value of being more wrong, it should go without saying that nobody should have to worry about being stigmatized for being wrong. Being wrong comes in many guises, and for many of them there is no major impact. If I make an attempt at a proposal and the client is not happy, it can be changed. If I handle a call in the wrong way, I can normally call back and recover the situation.

However, there are boundaries that will carry a certain stigma when crossed. This applies in the area of the language and vocabulary we use and is beyond the need to be merely politically correct. I have recounted how disturbed and offended I was when a friend voiced some unexpectedly racist views. My first thought was to withdraw from the friendship. I made the difficult decision to address my issues with the individual instead.

Whether it is views on race, religion, politics, gender, culture, or the concept of fairness, there are times when one statement or action can stain an individual in the eyes of the people who see or hear it. In theory, in an open environment, someone who says something inappropriate can be challenged and will be willing to learn. When it comes to people expressing views that deviate from the organization's or society's values—for example, making unconsciously biased comments—I'd argue that it's better for them to be challenged, or educated, in the open air or safe environment than to be silenced in one context and allowed to continue unchecked outside that context. This is a difficult one for many organizations because we often feel that we deserve not to listen to views we find unpleasant, hostile, or demeaning. But for a leader who seeks openness, papering it over with silence is not an option. Everyone has to be allowed to be wrong, verbally or in action, at least the first time. When someone repeats a mistake or fails in the same way, then it's time to question why that is. Society changes, values change, and the people we interact with change. Tolerance and the ability to listen, discuss, and learn together in the spirit of growth is the true definition of being refreshingly direct and acting as the Catalyst. In his book *Rebel Ideas: The Power of Diverse Thinking*,

Matthew Syed recounts the impact a woman called Allison had on the former KKK youth leader Derek Black in helping him change his deeply held views on race and religion. She was introduced to Black by her flatmate Matthew Stevenson, an Orthodox Jew in the same college, who invited Black despite his views to their hosting of Shabbat. Through a combination of empirical and researched work and Stevenson's bravery, they changed Black's views and helped him become a champion of racial equality. It's a very powerful story that illustrates that even in the worst situation of being wrong, there is a way to learn and unlearn in equal measure.

So What? Coach

Suggested System: Your Own Coaching System

So many people go into coaching because they feel it is giving back. But they are not practicing what they preach. There is nothing more compelling to others than their coach role-modeling the system of being coached and seeking coaching. Create a circle of coaches who really push you and stretch your learning. Share those stories. To be a coach, you have to be humble. Leaving your ego at the door and seeking help is a great step.

Suggested Habits

1   Start each conversation with "What's on your mind?" MBS's question serves me well as a habit. It sets a great tone.

2   Create the jigsaw in front of them: I find that taking notes as I coach is a great way to stay focused on the coachee. Switching my mind to creating a jigsaw of what the coachee is saying allows me to be their mirror and show them their thoughts.

3   Set a tone of humility: Being humble and admitting failings sets a good tone for others to see being more wrong as positive. Sharing when you have failed and what you struggle with shows strength they can learn from.

Part Five

what next?

11

your journey
continues

THE SYSTEMS AND habits of the leader are focused on the infinite game—not the short-term, finite game. The leader has to build systems and habits that are sustainable and adaptable to the challenges of the future. It is the start of a life's work for the leader.

So where do you start after reading this book?

Stop, pause, reflect, engage. When we return from attending a learning conference, my COO Sharon Hardcastle reminds us that our heads are full of "amazing shiny objects." The first step when you are in that mode is to stop, pause, and reflect for a while before engaging. Give yourself at least a week to process. I encourage you to do that with this book, too, and let your enthusiasm, new ideas, and thoughts on the systems, habits, and enablers you have read about in the book sink in. When you are ready to take things forward, then engage.

Do a leadership audit. While you let the ideas and thoughts sink in, conduct a leadership audit. You have probably been mentally measuring yourself against Pi2, anyway. Use your initial reactions to get out from behind your desk and start to observe your leadership through others' eyes. Use the Design Thinking questions: "What do they like?" "What do they wish was different?" "What do they wonder about?"

Conduct an audit on your leadership health in the context of the systems and habits we have talked about. Get others to share their observations and insights on you. Share those observations and insights with others to validate that they are true and useful.

If the support from your existing ecosystem is not immediately obvious, then choose a professional Catalyst to help you on your way. The measure of the leadership Net Promoter Score ("Would you recommend this person as a leader to others?") will be a strong indicator of where you sit in their minds. "What Do You Think of Me?" is a data-based exercise that will give you a baseline of where you sit. If you want to, take the Pi2 Leadership Assessment and get yourself a baseline report to work on. Then start to build your purposeful practice, one habit and one system at a time.

Review the "So What?" suggestions. Pick three to practice: it could be to work on your purpose, to try out a new identity, to be more curious about those around you, or to keep a journal or blog about your own leadership. You can start wherever it suits you best or with whatever motivates you most.

Work on your purpose. Start the process of crafting your stories from your life and career. Remember that the source of your purpose will be in the stories of what you are passionate about. Once you have crafted the "ugly" first version, sail it out of the harbor to test with people who care passionately for you—and maybe ones who are ambivalent or don't rate you. Explore and test your purpose.

Step over the threshold. The first step is always the hardest, whether it is to step into something or step back from something. Leadership is about embarking on the journey. Focus on small steps and small experiments in your life. Change the way you start your day. Change the way you end your day. Start a new way of working with your key stakeholders and clients. Take that walk in Nepal, write that book, post that letter, or send that email to explore a grant for a new business.

Capture your story. I started this book as a way of giving coherence to my own leadership journey, sparked a little bit by the wish that my grandparents, parents, and people like Randy Taylor, from whom I learned so much, had recorded theirs to allow me to read them. In sailing this ship out of the harbor, I believe that it will provide a spark to light a fire or fires in (or under) others. Their journey and your journey will be unique, but we will all have one thing in common: that we are OK with being more wrong.

epilogue

AND SO THE journey continues. Just as for Frodo and Harry Potter, the story is not over; the next stage in the journey is about to play out. In Frodo's case, he takes the last ship to the West, leaving Sam and Aragorn and the rest of his followers to lead the next chapters of the story in Middle-earth. Harry, Hermione, and Ron are seen waving goodbye to their children as they start their own adventures on the Hogwarts Express.

This stage in my journey may be at an end, but remember: This is an infinite game. Life as a leader is a lifelong journey of purposeful practice and always learning. Being more wrong is about getting up every morning excited about the day's experiment. What am I going to do today to learn fast? What seas am I going to sail in today with my followers? In fact, there is no end and what happens next in your journey is up to you.

I spent my early life wishing that I lived in another time and that life would give me something better than the challenges and rough seas I was sailing through. When I think about that now, I remember a conversation between Frodo and Gandalf in *The Lord of the Rings: The Fellowship of the Ring*:

"I wish it need not have happened in my time," said Frodo.

"So do I," said Gandalf, "and so do all who live to see such times. But that is not for them to decide. All we have to decide is what to do with the time that is given us."

What will you do with your time? What adventures do you want to have?

references

Barry, Dave. *Dave Barry Turns 50*. Crown, 1998.

Black, Jack. *MindStore: The Classic Personal Development Program*. Balloon View, 2015.

Brailsford, Sir Dave, and Chris Froome. Introduction to *The Pain and the Glory: The Official Team Sky Diary of the Giro Campaign and Tour Victory*, by Team Sky. Harper Sport, 2013.

Bungay Stanier, Michael. *The Advice Trap: Be Humble, Stay Curious & Change the Way You Lead Forever*. Page Two, 2020.

———. *The Coaching Habit: Say Less, Ask More & Change the Way You Lead Forever*. Page Two, 2016.

Cain, Susan. *Quiet: The Power of Introverts in a World That Can't Stop Talking*. Penguin, 2013.

Clear, James. *Atomic Habits: An Easy & Proven Way to Build Good Habits & Break Bad Ones*. Random House, 2018.

———. "The Beginner's Guide to Deliberate Practice." JamesClear.com, jamesclear.com/beginners-guide-deliberate-practice.

Covey, Stephen R. *The 7 Habits of Highly Effective People*, 30th anniversary ed. Simon & Schuster, 2020.

Doerr, John. *Measure What Matters: OKRs—The Simple Idea That Drives 10x Growth*. Portfolio/Penguin, 2018.

Duhigg, Charles. *The Power of Habit: Why We Do What We Do, and How to Change*. Random House, 2013.

Dweck, Carol. *Mindset: The New Psychology of Success*. Ballantine, 2007.

Edmondson, Amy C. *The Fearless Organization: Creating Psychological Safety in the Workplace for Learning, Innovation, and Growth*. Wiley, 2019.

———. "How Fearless Organizations Succeed." *strategy+business*, November 14, 2018. strategy-business.com/article/How-Fearless-Organizations-Succeed.

Ferriss, Tim. *Tools of Titans: The Tactics, Routines, and Habits of Billionaires, Icons, and World-Class Performers*. Houghton Mifflin Harcourt, 2016.

Fogg, B. J. *Tiny Habits: The Small Changes That Change Everything*. Virgin, 2019.

Gladwell, Malcolm. *Outliers: The Story of Success*. Penguin, 2009.

Goyder, Caroline. *Gravitas: Communicate with Confidence, Influence and Authority*. Vermilion, 2014.

Grant, Adam. *Give and Take: Why Helping Others Drives Our Success*. W&N, 2014.

———. (@AdamMGrant). "Psychological safety is a culture of respect, trust, and openness where it's not risky to raise ideas and concerns." Twitter, January 20, 2019, 9:34 a.m. twitter.com/adammgrant/status/1086995485934665730?lang=en.

Ibarra, Herminia. "The Authenticity Paradox." *Harvard Business Review*, January–February 2015. hbr.org/2015/01/the-authenticity-paradox.

Ismail, Salim. "Implications of Exponential Organizations." In *Exponential Organizations: Why New Organizations Are Ten Times Better, Faster, and Cheaper Than Yours (and What to Do about It)*, by Salim Ismail, with Michael S. Malone and Yuri van Geest. Diversion Books, 2014.

Katzenbach, Jon R., and Douglas K. Smith. *The Wisdom of Teams: Creating the High-Performance Organization*. McGraw-Hill, 2005.

Kelley, Tom, and David Kelley. *Creative Confidence: Unleashing the Creative Potential within Us All*. HarperCollins, 2015.

Klein, Gary. "Performing a Project Premortem." *Harvard Business Review*, September 2007. hbr.org/2007/09/performing-a-project-premortem.

Maister, David H., Charles H. Green, and Robert M. Galford. *The Trusted Advisor*. Simon & Schuster, 2002.

Marquet, L. David. *Leadership Is Language: The Hidden Power of What You Say—and What You Don't*. Penguin Random House, 2020.

McChrystal, General Stanley, with Tantum Collins, David Silverman, and Chris Fussell. *Team of Teams: New Rules of Engagement for a Complex World*. Portfolio/Penguin, 2015.

Miller, Donald. *Building a StoryBrand: Clarify Your Message So Customers Will Listen*. Thomas Nelson, 2017.

Milne Rowe, Sara. *The SHED Method: The New Mind-Management Technique for Achieving Confidence, Calm and Success*. Penguin, 2018.

Nachmanovitch, Stephen. *Free Play: The Power of Improvisation in Life and Art*. TarcherPerigee, 1991.

Newport, Cal. *Deep Work: Rules for Focused Success in a Distracted World*. Piatkus, 2016.

Obama, Barack. *A Promised Land*. Viking, 2020.

Pankhurst, Sylvia. *The Suffragette: The History of the Women's Militant Suffrage Movement*. Dover, 2015.

Ries, Eric. *The Lean Startup: How Constant Innovation Creates Radically Successful Businesses*. Portfolio/Penguin, 2011.

Scott, Susan. *Fierce Conversations: Achieving Success in Work & in Life, One Conversation at a Time*. Piatkus, 2017.

Sinek, Simon. "How Great Leaders Inspire Action." Filmed September 2009 in Puget Sound, WA. TEDx Talk video, 17:48. ted.com/talks/simon_sinek_how_great_leaders_inspire_action?language=en.

———. *The Infinite Game: How Great Businesses Achieve Long-Lasting Success*. Portfolio/ Penguin, 2019.

Smart, Jamie. *Clarity: Clear Mind, Better Performance, Bigger Results*. Capstone, 2013.

Syed, Matthew. *Black Box Thinking: Marginal Gains and the Secrets of High Performance*. John Murray, 2016.

———. *Rebel Ideas: The Power of Diverse Thinking*. Hodder & Stoughton, 2019.

Taleb, Nassim Nicholas. *Antifragile: Things That Gain from Disorder*. Penguin, 2013.

Tichy, Noel M. *The Leadership Engine: How Winning Companies Build Leaders at Every Level*. Harper Business, 2007.

Tolkien, J. R. R. *The Lord of the Rings: The Fellowship of the Ring*. HarperCollins, 1995.

Van Edwards, Vanessa. *Captivate: The Science of Succeeding with People*. Portfolio/ Penguin, 2018.

Varol, Ozan. *Think Like a Rocket Scientist: Simple Strategies for Giant Leaps in Work and Life*. WH Allen, 2020.

Watkins, Giles. *Positive Sleep: A Holistic Approach to Resolve Sleep Issues and Transform Your Life*. LID Publishing, 2019.

Klein, Gary. "Performing a Project Premortem." *Harvard Business Review*, September 2007. hbr.org/2007/09/performing-a-project-premortem.

Whitmore, Sir John. *Coaching for Performance: The Principles and Practice of Coaching and Leadership*, 5th ed. Nicholas Brealey Publishing, 2017.

Zielinski, Graeme. "J. Randolph Taylor, 72." *Washington Post*, January 9, 2002. washingtonpost.com/archive/local/2002/01/09/j-randolph-taylor-72/a8058 387-c89c-4b0a-9fab-b98f6e3e8032/.

about the author

COLIN HUNTER is an author, mentor, entrepreneur, coach, and CEO and lead guide of Potential Squared International, founded in 2001. Colin created Potential Squared to inspire leaders by disrupting the way they engage and develop their people. He and his global team specialize in creating immersive, measurable playgrounds to inspire new ways of thinking, systems, and habits. Colin's individual passion is for experimentation in leadership, creating impact through presence in leaders, and developing systems and habits embedded with purposeful practice for those leaders. Colin was born in Scotland but has lived in Newcastle, England; Paris, France; Hershey, PA; Montreat, NC; San Francisco, CA; and now resides in Aldbury, England. Among his many passions in life are cycling, traveling, soccer, and good food. He is married with two daughters.